## DATE DUE

| MAR 1 2002 | |
|---|---|
| MAR 1 9 2002 | |
| | |
| | |
| | |
| | |
| | |
| | |
| | |
| | |
| | |
| | |
| | |
| | |
| | |
| | |
| | |

BRODART                                    Cat. No. 23-221

Prisoner of the Emperor

# Prisoner of the Emperor

AN AMERICAN POW IN WORLD WAR II

Stanley W. Smith

*Duane A. Smith, editor*

UNIVERSITY PRESS OF COLORADO

Copyright © 1991 by the University Press of Colorado
P.O. Box 849
Niwot, Colorado 80544

10   9   8   7   6   5   4   3   2   1

The University Press of Colorado is a cooperative publishing enterprise supported,
in part, by Adams State College, Colorado State University, Fort Lewis College,
Mesa State College, Metropolitan State College of Denver, University of Colorado,
University of Northern Colorado, University of Southern Colorado,
and Western State College.

**Library of Congress Cataloging-in-Publication Data**

Smith, Stanley W., 1905–
    Prisoner of the Emperor: an American POW in World War II / Stanley W. Smith;
Duane A. Smith, editor.
        p.   cm.
    Includes bibliographical references and index.
    ISBN 0-87081-222-x
    1. Smith, Stanley W., 1905– .  2. World War, 1939–1945 — Prisoners and prisons,
Japanese.  3. World War, 1939–1945 — Personal narratives, American.  4. Prisoners
of war — United States — Biography.  5. Prisoners of war — Philippines — Biography.  I. Smith, Duane A.  II. Title.
    D805.P6S49   1991
    940.54′7252′095991 — dc20                                                    91-
29101
                                                                                  CIP

The paper used in this publication meets the minimum requirements of the
American National Standard for Information Sciences — Permanence of Paper for
Printed Library Materials. ANSI Z39.48–1984
∞

# Contents

# Foreword

... the generation that carried on the war has been set apart by its experience. Through our great good fortune, in our youth our hearts were touched with fire. It was given to us to learn at the outset that life is a profound and passionate thing.

Oliver Wendell Holmes, Jr., spoke these words at a Memorial Day gathering in Keene, New Hampshire, in 1884. They reflected his experiences in the Civil War, which had concluded nineteen years earlier. The eloquent, erudite Holmes summarized the feelings of generations of men before and since who marched off to war.

War experiences are not easy to write about. The stories arise from a need to express emotions that perhaps cannot be shared easily except with those who have had similar experiences. Stanley Westbrook Smith and his generation left their mark on a war that ended more than forty-five years ago and forever changed world history. It is his own story that he tells here, an exceptional account of a prisoner of war. It is a history that provides a sense of time, a sense of place.

In the original foreword to the journal, he states his goal in writing this account, which covers three years and ten months of his life:

One person's contribution to the war effort in World War II generally had no real bearing on the ultimate outcome, and the detailed experiences set forth in this narrative in no way violate that premise. My objective here, however, is to preserve information time has a way of eroding from memory. How kindly the material is treated over the years is not important, nor will it especially concern those of us who were granted the extraordinary privilege of returning to a rebirth of freedom.

The following pages fulfill this objective — the preservation of a segment of that war and one man's experiences when, in Holmes's words, "life was a profound and passionate thing."

DUANE A. SMITH

PHILIPPINES

LUZON

BATAAN

• CABANATUAN

CORREGIDOR • MANILA

TOKYO •

KOBE
•  • OSAKA

JAPAN

# Prologue

*Peaceful Nation at War.* So the Japanese have arrogantly set themselves up as the bosses of Asia. They have attacked this country in
one of the most treacherous assaults ever made in history. No doubt
can be felt as to the duty of the United States. Our people will
loyally support their government in the declaration of war which
Congress has passed. (Dec. 18, 1941)

Thus did the readers of the Sandwich, Illinois, *Free Press* learn of their
new wartime responsibilities. War had come to their world with the
attack on the naval base at Pearl Harbor, December 7, 1941, the Sunday
they would ever after know as "a date which will live in infamy"
(Franklin D. Roosevelt's war message to Congress, December 8, 1941).

Sandwich, a farming town of 2,608 on the main line of the Bur-
lington Railroad fifty some miles southwest of Chicago, was about as
isolated from the battlefront as any American community could be. Yet
war had reached even this hinterland. Five local young men promptly
enlisted after hearing the news of Pearl Harbor, and another, Stanley
W. Smith, was already stationed in the Philippines, the site of a major
Japanese attack and invasion.

Born in Sandwich on October 19, 1905, Smith grew up in the
community and graduated from the Loyola School of Dentistry in
1928. Establishing a profitable practice during the Depression in Mor-
ris, Illinois, proved slow and tedious. A career in the navy beckoned,
and in the fall of 1935 Smith was commissioned a lieutenant, junior
grade, in the Navy Dental Corps. With that move he started down the
path that would place him in Manila in December 1941. Following a
tour of sea duty at San Diego and shore duty at Great Lakes, Illinois,
he was ordered to join the Asiatic Fleet based at Manila, for which he
departed in August 1940. Tensions had already begun to mount between the United States and Japan, and the plans for his wife, Ila, and
their young son to accompany him were canceled.

The situation in the Far East was more critical than most Americans realized at the time, even though war had broken out in Europe
on September 1, 1939. The resulting battles and international tensions
as Nazi Germany surged to gain control of a continent had predictably

turned attention in that direction and away from other areas of the globe. Many Americans hoped their country would not become involved; those who believed it would, or should, looked with alarm at the deteriorating conditions in Europe and anticipated that war would come from that direction. It did not.

Meanwhile, the Japanese imperial government had continued its progress toward establishing what it proclaimed the "Greater East Asia Co-prosperity Sphere," in which Japanese political, economic, and military hegemony would be imposed upon Indochina, Thailand, the Dutch East Indies, and the Philippines. Although established as the major industrialized Asian nation, Japan lacked the natural resources to support its industry and status. The leaders, therefore, decided to look beyond the home islands for a solution. That decision had already involved Japan in two wars, one at the turn of the century with Russia, and the other in the 1930s with China.

The United States had emerged from the Spanish-American War in 1898 with a role in Asia: the Philippine Islands had fallen under its control. After crushing a short and bloody revolt there, the United States, to the amazement of other colonial powers, set about preparing the Filipinos for self-government and independence. Congress, after some hesitation, finally promised that July 4, 1946, would be the day this independence would be granted. As part of its program, the United States had built military bases and airfields to defend the Philippines and had established the capital and largest city, Manila, on Luzon Island, as the military keystone. It was considered by many to have the finest harbor in Southeast Asia and contained a major American naval base (including the Cavite Navy Yard, where Smith was assigned); several military airfields were located nearby.

The Japanese military studied these facts as they developed their plans. The Philippines, in themselves, were of no great economic importance except as a source of copper. Also, it was debatable whether the democratic and pro-American Filipinos would sympathize with the Japanese ambitions for East Asia. The islands remained, however, a threat to communications between Japan and one of its newly secured main targets, the oil fields in the Dutch East Indies.

As it unfolded in the years before the war, the Japanese plan was to neutralize the Pacific Fleet at the start of hostilities, deprive the United States of its base in the Philippines, and cut the line of communications across the Pacific by seizing Wake and Guam islands. The immediate objective of the strategy was the capture of the rich Dutch and British possessions; the attack on the Philippines would be merely a sideshow.

The American and Philippine governments had devised a defense strategy. They assumed that the Japanese would attack without a declaration of war; therefore, the initial defense would be conducted by American military and naval forces already stationed in the Philippines, supported by local troops. Their mission would be to hold central Luzon and Manila Bay until military relief could come from the United States. General Douglas MacArthur, who had earlier served as adviser to the Philippine Army, returned in July 1941 as Commander, United States Army Forces in the Far East. He saw this plan as a defeatist one. MacArthur wanted a more aggressive strategy and convinced both governments that a Japanese attack could be resisted and repelled. As fall became winter in 1941, he was devising new plans centered primarily upon the air force's launching of counterattacks.

Well aware of Japanese aspirations, the American, British, and Dutch governments had responded earlier in 1941 with economic sanctions on strategic materials. By summer of 1941 the Japanese had realized that they faced shortages of these crucial materials, shortages that would eventually weaken their economy. They faced a difficult choice: to surrender their ambitions or to take the offensive and risk war with all three countries. A war seemed less dangerous than the long-range alternative of bowing to foreign pressure. From a military point of view, the winter of 1941–42 offered an excellent opportunity for success, with the British and Dutch tied up in a European war.

The final Japanese plans for the seizure of the Philippines were completed in mid-November. The general scheme involved simultaneous air attacks on American airfields and installations on the first day, followed by landings to seize the airfields. The plan was based on detailed knowledge of the islands and a fairly accurate estimate of the number of American and Philippine forces.

The American military commanders had plenty of warning; for example, on November 27 a strong message came from Washington that an aggressive move was expected within the next few days. During the first week of December, American air reconnaissance, which was extended and intensified, observed heavy Japanese ship movements and unidentified planes, presumed to be Japanese, over Luzon.

News of the Pearl Harbor attack reached the Philippines early on the morning of December 8 (east longitude date). Still, Manila was taken by surprise when the first group of Japanese planes arrived shortly after noon and bombed Clark Field; within one day the Far Eastern Air Force was completely eliminated as an effective combat unit. Concerning this amazing development, World War II naval historian Samuel Eliot Morison wrote in 1963, "If surprise at Pearl Harbor is hard to understand, surprise at Manila is completely incomprehensible."

The major attack came two days later when the Cavite Navy Yard and a large part of the city of Cavite were destroyed. Nichols Field and other sites were also bombed. By December 12 the navy had lost control of the waters and the air surrounding Luzon; from December 8 through December 24, Japanese forces landed at various locations. American and Filipino troops were in retreat everywhere. Japanese objectives were being achieved to the fullest; indeed, the results were astounding.

MacArthur concentrated his forces on Bataan Peninsula and the island of Corregidor, following the plan that had been devised earlier. Unable to defend Manila and wishing to avoid its destruction by continued bombing, the withdrawing Americans declared it an open city on December 26; a week later the Japanese forces arrived.

During this time, Stanley Smith had managed to send three telegrams to his wife in Sandwich assuring her that he was safe and well. These would be his last messages for months. The narrative opens on December 7 (east longitude date), the last day of peace that he would know for three years and ten months.

D.A.S.

Prisoner of the Emperor

Chapter 1

# Red Sky in the Sunset

Sunday afternoon, December 7, 1941, in Manila, Philippine Islands, was a time of strange foreboding. I recall the usual bright tropical sun being obscured with low, overhanging clouds, and there was a stillness in the air suggesting some kind of change, a hint for the future, and the proper setting for the drama about to unfold in our part of the world. Actually on this particular afternoon I was in the Cavite area, more specifically at Canacao Naval Hospital located outside the navy yard. It is across the bay from Manila, some twenty kilometers more or less.

I, with two other naval dental officers, Lynn Wanger and Mahlon Fraleigh, living at the time in one of the pleasant quarters at Canacao, decided it was a good afternoon for a walk. Sangley Point, a naval air station in the process of construction, was our objective; it extended out from Canacao Hospital into Manila Bay. It is here I wish to begin my narrative.

Quite naturally the conversation turned to the possibility of war, for we were living in a continual state of crisis in the Far East. Recent information reported the admiral's staff expecting things to "break" hourly. The Asiatic Fleet, limited as it was in both size and effectiveness, had been ordered out of Manila Bay some seven or eight days earlier; we were on alert. Upon stepping ashore in San Francisco a few weeks before, an admiral who had recently been on duty in the area boldly told newspaper reporters, "We are ready in the Far East; our instruments are sharp!"

Although he spoke with such assurance, his opinion was given while his feet were firmly planted on good old U.S. soil. At best it must have been a tongue-in-cheek observation, or a clever bit of naivete. We with the so-called sharp instruments would have many occasions during the next three-and-some years to wish we had been fortunate enough to have gone ashore with the admiral. And what about those sharp instruments?

Foremost, and probably most likely to prove important in the long days ahead, was a certain indomitable spirit — something we Americans have always proudly acclaimed — a heritage that no invading force could take away from us by threat. I was to find out later the Japanese were to rely heavily upon this same quality of spirit for their ultimate success in this war that was about to unfold. At the time, none of us were about to give this "Nip" (as we then were referring to him) credit for any such inherent characteristic; later we were to have some second thoughts about the matter.

I must not let myself be carried away with enthusiasm, delving into the war before describing our Sunday afternoon walk and talk. Fraleigh did not agree that the Nipponese were serious in their threats, but Wanger and I concurred that they were indeed. We believed the Japanese this time had swaggered so arrogantly that to save face, so important to them, they were now caught in the embarrassing position of having either to fight or face national humiliation. If we didn't meet their demands, this time Nippon was going to fight.

In Fraleigh's opinion the State Department should continue to show a firm hand; we could outmaneuver them. This opinion was naive, yes, but not in view of what we were inclined to think concerning them. With our unlimited resources, unparalleled industry, reputation for never having participated in a losing war, and a fighting navy built on a "don't give up the ship" tradition, why shouldn't we stand firm in the face of what we regarded as saber-rattling by a much weaker opponent?

How well equipped was Japan conceded to be? It was "reliably" reported, and was the subject of general conversation throughout the Asiatic Fleet, that her aviators presently were not, and wouldn't ever be, first-class pilots. They did not have a good bomb sight, their air force was small, and their plane production was limited and for the most part obsolete. Their navy would be a cinch for us; in fact naval personnel here estimated we could probably knock off Japan in about six weeks, an opinion held by the serving commodore in command of destroyers. With an effective blockade, Japan wouldn't be able to go up or down the China Sea, her supply line would be broken, and she would be forced to her knees. This was the tenor of conversation in the wardroom of the ship to which, until recently, I had been assigned.

We rationalized that Japan would bypass the Philippines: we were far too formidable here; she would never be able to make a landing. However successful she was on some isolated point, we could, if necessary according to revised plans, retire to the Bataan Peninsula and across to Corregidor, where we could hold out indefinitely. Corregidor was impregnable, honeycombed with tunnels impervious to shelling. In any case artillery would not be brought to bear on the island, for we would expect to hold Bataan, making attack impossible. Perchance there were military men out here who didn't believe all this, but if so their feelings were well masked, and the more outspoken had already been transferred.

Fraleigh remarked, "Let me get duty in one of those caves on Bataan when this thing breaks; then they can blast away. That's the spot I want." Corregidor, "the Rock," as we so confidently referred to it, sounded like the best place to me. It was called the Gibraltar of the Far East, and although I had only passed it coming in and out of the entrance to Manila Bay, it looked very formidable, providing a quieting reassurance.

This was the general tone of our conversation while resting on Sangley Point. What did the air station there offer? Well, mostly some very plush, newly constructed barracks for officers and naval aviation personnel who would soon be assigned there. I am confident millions of appropriated dollars went into their construction. The airfield was in the process of being built, and already there were several oil dumps located in the area. Old PBY planes were anchored in the bay and lined up on the beach.

We observed several three-inch World War I vintage antiaircraft guns guarding this piece of U.S. property. We looked in vain for a five-inch AA gun, knowing these limited-range, smaller pieces could be effective only as moral persuaders. But then, we concluded, the Army Air Force from Clark Field wouldn't let planes get close enough to bomb. Someone had observed five-inch guns being unloaded in the port area. Lots of formidable military pieces were now being taken off incoming ships, but old Father Time was unalterably deciding the issue, and the Japanese, realizing time was running out, were not about to procrastinate any longer as we fortified our positions.

All three of us finally agreed we didn't have much in the Philippines. Possibly what we had was sharp, but terribly old in point of time and effectiveness. Initially Fraleigh thought we would be pushovers for the Japanese. I couldn't go along with that, for I had observed what appeared to be very impressive U.S. Army aircraft flying over Manila in those days: B–17s and fast-flying P–40s. The situation didn't look hopeless, and I was naive enough to conclude it just could not happen here. Of course we knew the Asiatic Fleet was a suicide squad, but the bulwark of our powerful offense as well as our main-line defense potential was located safely at Pearl Harbor, ready to weigh anchor at a moment's notice.

We returned to our Canacao quarters about sundown, and I popped some corn Ila had sent. It is a favorite of mine, which did not appeal to the rest of the fellows, so I looked forward to enjoying the remainder of it from time to time. Wanger and Fraleigh went to the station movies; I stayed at home in the semiblackout then in effect. Lights everywhere had to be hooded, with only a minimum of lighting allowed. Then to bed, a comfortable one I should have enjoyed this night, for it was about the last time I was to sleep in a bed when the only hindrance to sleep would be fighting off some vicious Canacao mosquitoes.

Before retiring I remember completing a lengthy letter to Ila and Duane, one I had started before leaving Baguio, where I had been on ten days' leave. In it I told all about the new quarters I had just been assigned at Canacao. The letter was never mailed and was later destroyed because it contained some uncomplimentary remarks about our enemies that would have been embarrassing, to say the least, for one in my position under the circumstances very soon to develop.

### PEARL HARBOR ATTACKED
### AND WE PREPARE FOR THE WORST

The interval of peace was distressingly short. The junior supply officer from the navy yard came by our quarters the following morning (Monday) at 7:00 A.M., short of breath and obviously carried away with excitement. He told us the Japanese had bombed Pearl Harbor, we were at war, and to get on the ball! None of us were particularly surprised, but the boldness of the attack amazed us; no one had even entertained the thought of such a desperate move on their part.

The explosive situation we had all theorized about, debated, and discussed during the past fifteen months I had been on duty in the Far East had finally arrived. The next several days would disclose our ultimate fate in the Philippines, for now it was generally conceded we would be next in the enemy offensive. The first blow at Oahu began a slow but sure undermining of the confidence I had entertained about our future. We tried to rationalize the attack on Pearl Harbor as not being as devastating as it sounded when first reported, but it was disturbing enough to create a feeling of doubt; perhaps our supply line — not that of the Japanese — would be severed, depriving us of the help necessary to hold off an invasion. However, our American birthright, that indomitable spirit we inherited, continued to sustain us.

I recall there wasn't much breakfast consumed, and we didn't lose time getting to our offices, Lynn and I to the yard dispensary, Mahlon to the hospital. At the dispensary the senior dental officer, along with the rest of us, took stock of our situation in light of what had already happened and what was likely to happen. The dispensary, a large, wooden frame building, and the dental clinic, a separate but much smaller wooden structure, were located in the very heart of the Cavite yard, directly in the middle of a potential inferno if we were bombed. Every building in the yard was constructed of wood and located in a congested area flanked on one side by the bay and ammunition depot and on the other by the nearby nipa-palm native village of Cavite. A more vulnerable spot for an air attack could hardly have been designed.

Directly behind the dental clinic was a relatively large old dungeon, partially underground, used in days of Spanish occupancy as some type of stockade, I suspect. It was of adobe construction and had a stone wall some fifteen feet high surrounding it. This wall, a good two feet in thickness, stood about thirty feet behind our office and the medical dispensary. We were novices at building air-raid shelters in those days — as we were about lots of things — but we were especially naive about the one put together behind our office to be used by dental personnel in case of an air attack: a few feet away from one side of the old prison enclosure, the yard workmen built a double wall about eight feet high and roughly fifteen feet in length, using one-inch pine boards. Between the two pine walls a six-inch space was left to be filled with sand. Crouching behind this construction was to be our air-raid "shelter" in case of enemy action: this makeshift wall was supposed to protect us from bombs.

Inexperienced as we were about such things, the dental department viewed the situation with a jaundiced eye, and we decided we didn't want to risk being toasted to a crisp or blown to bits, wedged between those flimsy boards and the insurmountable stone wall. We were convinced of an imminent raid and agreed not to be caught in any such fire trap. Many similar shelters were built around the yard for general use in this veritable tinderbox, all primed for a Nipponese bomb that wasn't long in arriving.

We were summoned to the armory on Monday morning, where in a state of general confusion we were outfitted with .45s — belt, gun clips, and all. This was contrary to the Geneva Convention ruling, which classified medical personnel as noncombatant, but I must admit the excitement of wearing a .45 appealed to me. We weren't fully aware of the potentialities of our predicament yet, although apprehension was building at a rapid rate. Steel helmets were also issued, and we were instructed to carry them at all times. The .45 felt somewhat reassuring on my hip, although it proved to be a nuisance later when maneuvering through small places during air raids. Fortunately I never had occasion to use it, but I did carry it faithfully, if somewhat clumsily, until the occupation forces were due to arrive in Manila.

The gas mask situation was amusing — even under prevailing circumstances. Peculiarly, everyone seemed certain some type of gas would be used during the war. This conviction was probably an aftermath of World War I and the postwar predictions and expectations about the use of poisonous gas in another world conflict. We were all in a frenzy to have a mask assigned — everyone except Dr. Lambert, the medical officer given the task of distributing them to the medical and dental departments. Slow and deliberate by nature, Dr. Lambert hadn't moved quickly enough with the distribution, and our senior dental officer, Dr. Neal Cross, who subscribed to the theory of having things done immediately (or sooner, if it could be arranged), proceeded to blow his top.

We were now experiencing periodic air-raid alarms throughout the day and night, the wailing sirens sending out their ominous warning over the Manila area. The senior medical officer of the navy yard dispensary, Lt. Comdr. Hjalmar Erickson, ordered Wanger and me to set up and maintain an emergency dressing station at Porta Vaga, a small, old Spanish building located inside one entrance gate in the original wall surrounding Cavite. Apparently at one time, during Spanish rule in the Philippines, walls were constructed around all areas of Spanish occupancy as a protection from native attacks. These walls remain today, for the most part, at various points in and around Manila.

Within Manila itself is the venerable Walled City (Intramuros), entirely surrounded by a high, twelve-foot-thick wall, with various observation points at strategic positions and elaborate portals of entry located on all sides. Originally, a moat completely surrounded the Walled City; the depression for it still remains, although army engineers cleaned out the mosquito-infested place when we took over the Philippines at the turn of the century. Now a nice grass parkway encircles it, even though the old stores, churches, and dwellings inside are located amid general conditions of uncleanliness, with little evidence of proper sanitation. A most interesting place, however, and many of my hours ashore until now had been spent browsing in the intriguing Chinese and Filipino shops inside.

Almost all the things I had sent home to Ila and Duane came from Walled City vendors. I regretted having withheld some purchases I now would never send home to them. One of particular attraction was the little, fat, captivating ivory Buddha that sat on my desk laughing at me all day long with an impish grin that, interpreted properly during the time I possessed it, no doubt was trying to tell me something. I was annoyed at having to lose him and his inveigling smile.

My Bali heads were two of the finest I had seen out here; I spent many pleasant hours wrangling over the purchase price and inevitable cumshaw from the Chinese merchant. I forget how many days it took me to finally close the deal, but it was all enjoyable nevertheless and was helpful in passing many otherwise lonesome hours. I should have mailed the heads home; I suspect I became too attached to them, and now of course they would be lost forever.

AIR-RAID ALARMS INTENSIFY

I must get back to the primary concern, the war. Lynn and I took many of the dressings and drugs considered necessary to our assigned battle station at Porta Vaga and equipped it as completely as we were able. Air-raid alarms continued with greater frequency, sounding dire warnings of things to come. We had several throughout the day (Monday). One current rumor circulating predicted the bombing of the navy yard at noon the following day. Rumors, of course, were prevalent everywhere, and as a result we were kept in a continual state of tension. One of the first official reports received described the loss of the USS *Prescott*, destroyer aviation tender of the Asiatic Fleet, carrying high-test gasoline. It was reported lost by enemy action in Philippine waters, including all hands aboard — not difficult to believe with such a cargo.

During these early days I was congratulating myself on having been transferred to Manila from the USS *Blackhawk* on November 24. I had jokingly told my shipmates on board how the Japanese one day would blow them out of the water while I would be sitting in comparative safety on dry land in the navy yard. Right now, in recalling the conversation, it didn't seem so amusing. The response presented by my shipmates featured a few well-placed bombs wiping out the yard completely, leaving me, if still alive, eating rice and fish in a Japanese prison camp. In light of what was happening I began to weigh their remarks more seriously; as it turned out their only miscalculation was the reference to having fish as a part of my diet.

I didn't view the subject quite so flippantly now; however, the time hadn't yet arrived when I would have exchanged places with them. A destroyer tender, the *"Hawk"* had a top speed of eleven knots, no armament, antiquated six-inch guns, and appeared to me as a classic example of a sitting duck. My change of duty orders had been approved by the fleet medical officer, and I would have been on my way to relieve the dental officer at Peking, China, this very moment had not the marines been pulled out, causing my orders to be canceled. I would have liked that assignment very much, so I thought, but as long as I couldn't have the duty there, I was presently satisfied to be at the navy yard and not on the *Blackhawk*.

Word arrived after an air-raid alarm at noon on Monday that Clark Field, about one hundred or so kilometers north of Manila, had been heavily bombed during the lunch hour. We didn't at first hear how successful the attack had been; however, the reported plane loss did sound discouraging. It was difficult to believe, with all the experience gleaned from similar action in Europe, that we could get caught with planes on the ground. Nichols Field, at the edge of Manila — in fact not far from us — was the other army airfield in this area. We were now convinced the navy yard at Cavite would be high on the Nipponese list of objectives. Our P–40s and an occasional P–38 were zooming overhead most of the time, but losses at Clark would be severely felt, for, if initial reports could be relied upon, we were apparently hurt badly.

The first night after becoming actively engaged in the war, we retired at the end of a long day with the seriousness of the situation closing in upon us. It was, however, a beautiful tropical evening: a full moon without a cloud in the sky — the time of year out here when the weather is perfect. It is logical to surmise that the Japanese had taken this into consideration when they opened their offensive. Excitement was too great to remember the sunset on this particular evening, but they are consistently of such exquisite beauty, with such brilliantly flaming colors, that even the stepped-up tempo of the war couldn't dim our appreciation of this spectacular display. I am confident there is no place in the world where sunsets are more indescribably beautiful.

I turned in about midnight; Wanger, Fraleigh, and Bob Hearthneck, the other dental officer who had now moved in with us, continued to rehash the day's events. Excitement so permeated the atmosphere wherever people congregated that it became increasingly difficult to relax sufficiently to sleep. We had dropped by one of the other officer's quarters during the blackout and listened to the shortwave broadcast from KGI, San Francisco. The ether was full of threats, counterthreats, and statistics. The ones we were hearing from KGI we thought undoubtedly presented the true picture, for we were still under the impression our radio didn't have to put out propaganda to shore up confidence.

The damage reported at Pearl Harbor didn't appear to be heavy, although KGI was ambiguous about specific figures. Domei news agency from Tokyo, of course, was broadcasting striking successes scored against our fleet at Pearl Harbor: many ships had been irreparably damaged, others blown out of the water, and our naval forces hopelessly crippled. This was an obvious distortion of the facts no one out here was inclined to believe at the time.

### MANILA RECEIVES A WARNING HINT FOR THE FUTURE

About 12:30 A.M. the next morning (Tuesday), the air-raid alarm in Manila began wailing; our Cavite siren would join it shortly. It was a beautiful night for an air raid — even with a complete blackout, targets would be distinctly visible. No lights were allowed, so putting on our required paraphernalia presented difficulties; however, we succeeded somehow and the four of us went down by the breakwater off the hospital grounds. If anything were to happen, we would go to our battle stations; otherwise the breakwater offered a grand view of surrounding Manila and the whole bay area. In addition, the cement wall there afforded protection in the event some bombs were directed our way.

All appeared quiet over Manila. No lights could be seen, and except for occasional shouting in the distance — almost everybody gave directions in those days — nothing disturbed the moonlit beauty of the night. Perhaps a half hour went by, and we were seriously considering returning to our quarters when planes were heard in the distance. They of course could have been U.S. fighter aircraft, but we were inclined to think otherwise. Excited shouts grew more numerous as Manila stirred.

The approaching planes were now directly over us; we could see them quite plainly, although no running lights were showing. Several terrific explosions were heard in the direction we estimated to be Nichols Field, and almost as quickly as the sound reached us, we saw huge billows of smoke and flame shooting skyward. Actually there were not a great number of explosions, not many planes for that matter, and, incidentally, not much antiaircraft response challenging them.

Ugly-looking fires were now lighting the sky, and we reminded ourselves that Japanese pilots were not supposed to be capable of accurate bombing due to their sometimes held to be characteristic astigmatism. We were naive enough to quickly rationalize that some of their allies must have been manning the bomb sights. They made only one run in this raid, and, as nothing developed in the next hour, we decided to go back to bed. The navy yard and hospital did not appear to be objectives in tonight's attack.

We couldn't shake the feeling that this had been a brush with the real thing and a foretaste of more ominous happenings. Lynn, Mahlon, and I solemnly agreed we would remain together if we possibly could, whatever the circumstances before us; we felt a closer association now. In fact all of us experienced varied and disquieting reactions during those early days of the conflict. I suspect no matter how much preliminary preparation you make to meet an emotional crisis, when the event actually arrives, you are not adequately prepared to cope with all its ramifications. In this instance it was the feeling of being uprooted from the security we had always enjoyed and taken for granted; our way of life was in jeopardy. On this night, however, I was extremely tired and a bed was the most important thing I wanted to contemplate.

On Tuesday morning, the second day of the war, excitement was in the air everywhere. Last night's raid brought enemy action closer to us, creating quite an uproar at the yard. Now we were indeed more inclined to believe yesterday's rumor that we would be bombed today at noon. There was a strong feeling afloat that fifth-column radio-beam activity had guided the Japanese bombers to Nichols the night before. It sounded logical, for the bombing was reported to be very accurate, too accurate without assistance of some sort. There was a large Japanese population with questionable civilian status living in and around Manila. This morning they were in the process of being rounded up as a security measure.

An amusing incident occurred, a supplement to my earlier air-raid shelter story. The navy yard medical department wisely acquired the old Spanish dungeon located there as a combination shelter and main dressing station for casualties, planning and equipping it for any future eventualities. Conscientious Dr. Gordon Lambert was again detailed in charge, and after making all preparations, he proceeded to secure the first-aid facility with a big padlock — until such time as it would be needed, so he said. The prospect of coming upon a locked shelter during the near panic of an air raid, together with the unlikelihood of anyone being able to readily locate the key, was too much for those who would be affected. Someone promptly made away with both lock and keys.

Dental officers were now assuming a round-the-clock watch, so both Wanger and I spent the second night of the war on duty in the shelter trying to get some much needed sleep between air alarms. Although the rumored raid hadn't materialized, we were sure it was imminent. Wednesday morning we were worn out, so it was proposed that the dental clinic operate on a half-day schedule from now on. We left for our quarters on the hospital grounds for a morning's rest before returning for the afternoon shift. Our Filipino houseboy was a good cook, and I discovered nothing happening so far had in any way inhibited my appetite.

BOMBS OVER CAVITE

The air alarm sounded at 12:30 P.M., before we had quite finished lunch. The raids on the Philippines from the Japanese mainland usually followed a pattern, arriving at high noon or around midnight. We couldn't risk this one not being "for real," so we hurried to catch the 12:40 ferry bringing us across the bay to our dispensary offices. By the time we arrived at the ferry, however, it had suspended operation until the all-clear would sound, wisely fearing possible strafing during the ten-minute crossing. The drone overhead of approaching planes helped Lynn and me to make a quick decision to use the shelter at the waterfront on the hospital grounds, and we lost no time in hurrying back to this location, where many of the hospital staff would be. This shelter was a small replica of the one we had put into use at the navy yard.

The intensified roar indicating a large flight of planes was heard approaching from the north over Manila. They looked, from our position inside the shelter, like silver birds in the sky; under different circumstances, they would have been a beautiful sight. There was no question in anyone's mind now what was in store for us. They arrived in perfect formation directly over the navy yard in groups of ten or twelve, possibly 20,000 feet over the target; later estimates placed the total at approximately seventy planes.

Bursts of three-inch AA fire beneath them was agonizing to observe. Someone suggested throwing rocks might have been as effective; not a plane deviated from its course. We were chagrined not to see any of our fighters appear to challenge them; it was almost like observing flight training of our own bombers. The first squadron turned out to be a "dummy run," and we had the feeling their pilots were executing it with cool, calculated assurance that there would be no effective opposition, and much to our disappointment, there wasn't.

To be guilty of strange behavior when bombs are being directed overhead for the first time shouldn't be considered unusual. It is perfectly natural to expect to be frightened, and there was no one in the shelter with us who didn't qualify. In thinking about the raid after it was over, I was amused to recall some of the officers using blankets, and even mosquito nets, as additional protection over their heads when the bombs were exploding nearby. The first wave shook the old

Spanish enclosure to its foundation, and we knew the adjoining navy yard was receiving the brunt of it. We looked out to see flames and huge billows of black smoke shooting skyward over the whole area.

A marine in a small truck stopped outside the shelter, asking for volunteers to assist at the yard, so Lynn and I took advantage of the opportunity to go with him to our battle station at nearby Porta Vaga. It was a wild ride, I can assure you. We traveled at breakneck speed, with planes overhead and bombs exploding all around us, trying to avoid groups of Filipinos who were hurrying in all directions in the hope of finding some protection.

When we arrived at Porta Vaga, at the edge of the village of Cavite, we found casualties lying all around: Filipino civilian employees from the yard, as well as villagers who were caught in the holocaust, most of them severely burned from the explosions and the resulting fires. We began moving them into a nearby Catholic church. By now it seemed the bombing had been going on for hours, and we wondered if it ever would stop. It was obvious the fires were sweeping the entire yard facilities. Those unhurt created the most disturbance; their unrestrained shouting of meaningless directives and orders as they ran aimlessly about added greatly to the confusion. The ones to appear most calm and composed were the poor injured Filipinos, so many beyond any help we could give them.

As I reflect upon it the situation was indeed horrible, our assistance pitifully inadequate. We were two dental officers, operating alone under these circumstances, taxed beyond our professional knowledge and ability. I had never before been called upon, nor did I have the training, to do such extensive first-aid bandaging, splinting, ligating, and administering of medication for the relief of pain. Certainly I had never done it alone under such extreme conditions. We were soon out of bandages, out of drugs, out of ligatures, out of tourniquets — out of everything except casualties, and they kept pouring in, carried on their friends' shoulders and in their arms. What a sight, what a terrible, frustrating afternoon, but I was too emotionally drained to take much stock of its full significance.

Our initial resentment over what we considered to be a vicious, unwarranted attack brought to mind the desire for revenge. In sober afterthought the bombing had to be evaluated as a strategically conceived maneuver on a military objective — something to be anticipated by any people foolish enough to be at war. Why wasn't the navy yard evacuated before inevitable misery was brought down upon these poor people? The whole area was vulnerable and practically defenseless, almost every building a firetrap.

Marine gunners threw everything they possessed at the attacking planes. "Everything" in this instance amounted to .30- and .50-caliber machine guns, in addition to the .45s of those who became carried away in the excitement. Our battle station was located next to the ammunition depot, a most unlikely spot to be in case of a direct hit — fortunately at the time, it didn't enter our minds. I suspect the Japanese pilots knew its location very well and were hopeful of scoring a bull's-eye; many bombs were falling in the bay near the ammunition dump. A hit would have widened Manila Bay by another quarter of a mile, more or less, and suddenly terminated World War II for all of us.

As soon as it was possible, we commandeered every car, truck, and *calesa* (two-wheeled, horse-drawn carriage) in the area to transport patients to nearby Canacao Naval Hospital. We crowded every vehicle to the maximum, hoping to get the casualties there while our emergency treatment still sustained them. Many would succumb from the shock of severe injury, but how commendably brave and uncomplaining most of them were! We sent volunteers into every available drugstore not presently afire to take forcibly, if necessary, all surgical dressings and drugs they could find. Some establishments, we were told, resisted but were quickly convinced of their error.

I was relieved but extremely tired when the day was over. It was an afternoon that seemed like an eternity, but we were thankful to be alive. We began to ponder the welfare of our dispensary friends who had been on duty in the yard when the bombing began. Dr. Erickson arrived during the latter part of the raid, from where I don't know, but we were glad to see him, to have his help, and to know he was all right. He was more dazed than we and told of having witnessed the bombing from the breakwater and being blown into the bay by a nearby explosion. He had several pieces of shrapnel in his chest. Laney, a dental corpsman who was crouched by his side at the time, was killed with the same blast — at least he was last seen alive when it occurred.

Near midnight we were told to evacuate the yard as the fires were moving dangerously near the ammunition depot. With the sisters' help (I cannot remember which religious order they belonged to), we moved the last of the casualties from the church we had used as a temporary hospital and retired to the edge of Cavite in hopes of getting some sleep. What a day! What a classic example of man's inhumanity to man.

The next day we observed for the first time the utter confusion and panic accompanying an emergency evacuation. Many feared the bombers would return, and the remaining civilian population in Cavite was frantically leaving, going anywhere to get out of the area. Packing whatever was left of their worldly possessions in carabao carts, baby carriages, or any other wheeled vehicle, they crowded into the narrow roadways leading out of the village. Fortunately the patients from Canacao Hospital, which was now being abandoned, could be ferried across the bay to Manila and did not have to be moved through the frantic congestion of fleeing civilians crowding the highways to Manila.

Navy medical and dental personnel from the yard, together with the group from the abandoned naval hospital, were told to report to Sternberg Army Hospital in Manila. Arriving there we were temporarily quartered at Estado Mayor, wooden buildings adjoining Sternberg used mostly as storage space for excess military equipment. With emergency problems of their own, the army, I'm satisfied, was inclined to classify our navy group as "excess military equipment" as well. Sternberg Hospital, located in Manila proper, was a large, old hospital now jammed with bombing casualties. Our Canacao Hospital staff had convinced themselves Japanese bombers would return to destroy it. As it turned out we could have operated safely there, and with greater efficiency, until the fall of Manila.

It could be expected, this early in the war, to find everything in a most volatile state of utter confusion, and it was. Air raids in Manila were occurring several times a day now; the overall military picture in the Philippines wasn't encouraging and was steadily worsening. There appeared to be a general lack of organization and coordination all around us. If there had been a prearranged military plan for an emergency such as this, and I am sure one did exist, extenuating circumstances now made it obsolete. The term *snafu* to describe such a situation surely must have been coined during this particular period, it so aptly applied to the conditions confronting us in the Philippines.

A news item released by Admiral Hart's staff the day of the bombing worried some of us because it carried misinformation concerning our welfare. They reported all medical personnel attached to the navy, including patients in the yard dispensary, killed when the clinic received a direct hit. Our families at home would be unnecessarily alarmed, when in reality none of us were in the dispensary at the time it was bombed. The building did receive a direct hit, however, that would have wiped out anyone occupying it. Fortunately, those at the clinic when the alarm sounded scattered to other locations in the navy yard and adjoining areas.

With this added concern in mind, and realizing the time was rapidly approaching when it would be impossible for us to send messages home, I hurried to the telegraph office on the Escolta in Manila to cable my present safety to Ila and Duane. I am pleased that they did receive the message, although Ila's effort to send back a reply failed, through no fault of hers. Throughout the war the possibility of my message not having been received bothered me. Aware anything of value would be stripped from us in the event of capture, I also radioed some money to Ila from a Manila bank; a pay allotment I had previously made out would, of course, continue.

Capt. Robert Davis, our senior medical officer, ordered Dr. Cross, Wanger, and me to return to the yard on Saturday as part of a medical detail to help identify and bury the navy dead. This undoubtedly was the most gruesome task I was called upon to perform during the war. Between Wednesday and Saturday most of the fires had burned out, leaving charred ash and smoldering timbers. The stench of burned and decaying flesh was almost more than one could bear — certainly for any length of time. I don't know how many bodies and parts of bodies were uncovered in the debris; in fact I doubt whether accurate losses from the bombing were ever made known. Hundreds were uncovered, but hundreds of civilian workers and military were burned under falling buildings, leaving no trace.

Identification of those we uncovered proved nearly hopeless; the records were not available, and their poor shapeless bodies were burned beyond recognition in most cases. When we happened upon what was left of the dental office air-raid shelter, we found the charred remains of six poor civilian workers who had sought its sanctuary during the raid, a bitter confirmation of our earlier assessment.

As quickly as could be done — the foul odor was nauseating at times — the bodies were placed in bomb craters, where a short prayer was offered and the remainder of the crater filled in. Commander Strong, a line officer from the yard, was in charge. His job was most unpleasant, but he remained at it for many days, and he deserves the highest commendation for his work. I believe he suffered emotional disturbance for the remainder of the war directly related to this depressing task. It was that kind of a day, and a forerunner of more difficult ones to come for all of us.

During the next several days, Neal Cross, Lynn, and I used our commandeered truck between air raids, shuttling back and forth from Cavite and Canacao to Manila, helping to salvage the naval medical stores remaining in the supply depot located near the hospital. During a raid, with enemy planes overhead, we would stop alongside the road and try to hide in a nearby ditch for the duration of the alarm. I don't recall any strafing, but at times like this you foolishly imagine every plane coming over has its sights directed upon you personally.

Viewing the interior of the vacated navy hospital was an experience I will remember for many years to come. The patients and almost all of the equipment practical to move had been taken out. The rooms and hallways were littered and splattered from one end of the building to the other with blood-soaked bed linen, mattresses, and discarded surgical dressings — mute evidence of human suffering and death prevailing there as a result of the recent bombing. Nothing remained but the barren walls of a once-proud institution — a most discouraging sight.

### WE JOIN THE ARMY

Patients were arriving in ever-increasing numbers from the front lines established to stem the tide of the invading forces. Several landings on the islands had now been successful. Navy personnel, after many days of weary frustration at Estada Mayor, were finally divided into surgical teams and assigned to the army in field hospitals assisting with the care of battle casualties. Captain Davis, senior medical officer from Canacao, in the meantime had organized a temporary naval hospital at Balintawak, a small Seventh Day Adventist college at the edge of Manila. Dr. Erickson, a reserve officer who had been an Adventist physician on its staff, secured the use of the building for the navy. Not many of our medical personnel were needed there, so most of us were ordered to report to the army.

Fraleigh, Wanger, and I separated for the first time. Except for a few brief months, I wouldn't see Fraleigh again for the remainder of the war. Wanger was soon to join me at a later assignment. For the present I was ordered with Comdr. Clyde Welsh, MC, USNR, to Holy Ghost College, a Catholic institution at the edge of Manila proper, where we established a field hospital as part of an army team.

Holy Ghost was one of several Catholic schools in the Manila area being used for field hospitals. Captain Fox, a U.S. Army physician, was in command of ours; the navy personnel composed only a small part of the team. This field hospital operated until just before Manila fell. The rapid withdrawal of our forces prompted the army to vacate before it had qualified itself to any great degree. Happily for us the sisters were very kind, preparing and serving all our food in addition to washing all the hospital's and our personal laundry. We enjoyed deliciously prepared meals for the last time during the war, and in the months ahead I would have ample reason to recall their elegant quality on many occasions.

Daily bombing was rapidly reducing Manila to a city of ugly fires and many gutted buildings. Other than sporadic and ineffectual anti-aircraft fire there was no apparent opposition to these raids. No raid, however, was as devastatingly accurate as the navy yard attack. They were now consistently missing such targets as ships in the bay, the valuable and much-used port area docks, shipping in the Pasig River, and various oil refineries in Manila. I don't believe they deliberately bombed nonmilitary objectives, but many churches and buildings in that category were frequently hit as a result of their apparent inability to find their targets. Perhaps the first-line aviators had been transferred to more vital areas of combat.

Estada Mayor, where we had stayed temporarily, was one such building destroyed; some were inclined to believe the Japanese were directing their bombs at Sternberg Hospital, but more likely Estada Mayor's nearness to the shipping in the Pasig River accounted for its destruction. Santo Domingo Cathedral outside the Walled City was heavily damaged in one raid.

Early in the war during air raids we would retire to designated areas, with all our .45s, helmets, and gas masks, to wait out the all-clear siren. As the war progressed and the occupation of Manila became more imminent, we weren't so bomb-happy; we would stand on the balcony at Holy Ghost watching the planes come over, trying to estimate where the bombs were being dropped. We were convinced by now the pilots didn't know of our present location and probably could not care less.

Prior to the evacuation of Manila, the U.S. Army frantically tried to move the vast quantities of supplies stored in the large bodegas (warehouses) in the port area to the tunnels of Corregidor across the bay. The Japanese, on the other hand, were as frantically trying to bomb the storage facilities to destroy supplies helping to maintain our forces. Neal Cross, our explosive senior dental officer, had been ordered to join us at Holy Ghost, and he couldn't resist acquiring some of this clothing and food being trucked from the bodegas. So we ventured forth on another scrounging detail, loading tons of food and clothing in the small truck Neal had managed to latch on to, bringing it to our field hospital at Holy Ghost, where it was eventually left for the sisters.

We obtained all the stateside packaged food and other supplies time would allow, and when the Quartermaster Department finally vacated the port area, the Filipinos made quick work of what was left and, I suspect, in the lean months ahead would rejoice over the opportunity it had afforded. Amusingly enough in retrospect, Dr. Cross was inadvertently locked inside one of the bodegas during an air raid, and to say he was perturbed would indeed be a gross understatement.

Christmas Day, understandably, our morale dropped to a new low. It was the most depressing Christmas I had ever experienced. The sisters served sumptuous quantities of wonderfully cooked food, but I am afraid very few of us ate it with any enthusiasm. I had some recordings Ila sent of Duane's and her voices that I had managed so far to save and play whenever I had the opportunity. They provided the only bright spot in what was rapidly developing into a desolate, gloomy picture. I remember Duane's childish voice in one of the recordings saying, "Daddy, you come out of that old China!" How desperately I wished it were possible.

The army personnel with us had finally evacuated to either Bataan or Corregidor, leaving our navy team at Holy Ghost in charge of all remaining patients. Lynn Wanger and Commander Joses, MC, USN, arrived the day after Christmas, bringing us together again. They had been working in the port area, helping with the evacuation, and were left unattached when the remainder of the army, having been on duty in the defense of Manila, boarded the boat leaving with the last of the stragglers. We became more than mildly concerned with receiving navy orders to move out of Manila, transferring us to what we hoped would be the relative security of Corregidor, for eventual regrouping of our forces.

### MANILA BOWS HER HEAD

By now Manila had been declared an open city, and military installations of all descriptions had been removed. A pall of smoke hung over the entire area from the many smoldering fires visible for miles around. Some of the fires, of course, had been started by our retreating forces carrying out a policy of destroying installations and supplies that couldn't be moved and would be of use to the enemy. The Nipponese offensive was rapidly closing in on Manila, and the inevitability of the approach was reflected in the faces of the people you met on the street.

We decided the time had come to disarm, more nearly conforming to the Geneva Convention ruling establishing noncombatant status for all medical personnel. We made a ceremony of going to the edge of the Pasig River behind the now-deserted Malacanang Palace, throwing our guns, including an attractive little .32 caliber I had acquired, as far out into the river as we could. We anxiously awaited orders to leave, hoping to avoid the approaching occupational forces, for each night we remained in Manila lessened our chances of possible escape. Each day that dawned assumed a tremendous importance to our immediate future.

One evening at sundown Dr. Cecil Welch, one of the medical officers, and I walked across town to the Army-Navy Club near the Luneta for what turned out to be my last visit there. For the first time we learned from a naval intelligence officer how really serious the Pearl Harbor attack had been. Practically all the damage claimed by the Japanese radio had in fact been accomplished. This information didn't in any way bolster our morale during those dark days when confidence in the early arrival of reinforcements was being sorely tested. I had previously moved all my Philippine possessions, except what I could carry in a duffel bag, to permanent storage in the club; I now began to speculate about how much of it the Japanese would find useful.

The navy group at Balintawak Temporary Hospital had now been moved back into Manila, occupying Santa Scholastica College, recently evacuated as a field hospital by the army. We carried out orders from Captain Davis to leave Holy Ghost, reporting to Scholastica to rejoin the Canacao Hospital Command several days before New Years. Although disappointed at not being offered the sanctuary of Corregidor, we were relieved to be rejoining what was left of our navy in Manila, especially now that only stragglers of the military remained there.

Trying to make the most of our remaining days of freedom, several of us out walking on one occasion came upon a gathering of U.S. civilians at one of the government buildings, who were residing in Manila at the time of the Japanese invasion. Their helplessness and near panic was appalling. I couldn't, however, resist the feeling they were caught in a situation of their own choosing, having been amply warned earlier to leave the Philippines. Their spokesman had been frantically sending messages to nearly everyone of importance in the States, urging that arrangements be made for their safe evacuation. It points out the tendency, so often observed during periods of emotional stress, to look elsewhere for responsibility involving one's own poor judgment.

New Year's Day arrived, and with it our last hope of receiving official orders to leave Manila vanished. The city was surrounded, awaiting the triumphal entry of the invading armies. We were left to face whatever the Japanese decided should be our fate; our future was most precarious, depending upon their will and pleasure. There was a wide range of speculation amongst ourselves about what we could expect. We had confirmed reports from the front lines that neither side had accepted prisoners, an ominous implication. We recalled the earlier mass executions by the Japanese in China. One of our patients, a lieutenant commander of the line, gripped with despondency over the situation, jumped to his death from the top of the highest Scholastica building on New Year's morning, landing a few feet from where I was standing. The most optimistic of us held that the best we could hope was to become prisoners of war of the Japanese emperor, whatever that entailed.

Capt. Robert Davis, medical officer in command, called a conference of all hands to remind us the war was over as far as any active participation on our part was concerned. His last orders, received about December 20 from the admiral of the 16th Naval District, had been to maintain a hospital in Manila. We had complied to the best of military tradition, but now we were to become pawns of an enemy whose precedent, under circumstances similar to ours, was unpredictable. Anyone, so we were told, who was harboring an intention to leave, proceeding on his own initiative, would be classified as a deserter by Davis. This warning came as a surprise, although I am confident very few, if any, were courageous enough to actually attempt such a move; at least I knew of no medical personnel who admitted to such a plan.

Our one hope remained; it would only be a matter of weeks until reinforcements would permit General MacArthur to retake Manila and secure our release. The most pessimistic among us were saying it might be months instead of weeks, but theirs was regarded as a defeatist attitude. To those of us who persevered to the end, we could always move the dateline ahead as one optimistic prediction after another failed to materialize. In general, this was the philosophy that would keep us from the depths of despair and sustain us throughout the lengthy duration of an imminent incarceration.

# Chapter 2

# Magnanimity of the Emperor

With the military abandonment of Manila, the Philippine campaign dissolved into a slow retreat on Bataan. Because the Japanese had gained complete aerial and naval supremacy, the only hope of MacArthur's ground forces lay in fighting a delaying action until help arrived. No help would come; the remaining American army and navy units were expendable.

President Franklin Roosevelt ordered MacArthur to leave for Australia, which he did in March; Gen. Jonathan Wainwright assumed command. After Bataan was evacuated on April 8, the remnants of the American and Filipino forces dug in at Corregidor, the Rock. For another month they held out, but the bitter moment came on May 6 when Wainwright surrendered. The Philippine campaign was over.

This, the greatest surrender in American military history, concluded a series of disasters that had begun six months before at Pearl Harbor. It had not been all in vain, however, this Philippine campaign. The troops had denied Manila Bay to the enemy, slowed down the Japanese by forcing them to use more men and planes than intended, inflicted heavy casualties, and given Americans the epic struggles of Bataan and Corregidor around which to rally. The troops' fate had been decided on the opening day of the war when the Pacific Fleet had been so badly damaged at Pearl Harbor, making relief impossible. But they fought on, proving that the Japanese were not invincible.

Manila, a prewar city of 623,000, and its strategic harbor now lay in the hands of the Japanese. For Smith and the other prisoners, this was a period of trying to adjust to life in a prisoner-of-war camp. Smith learned very early an interesting aspect of his new situation as a POW dentist: "various Nipponese military . . . began to avail themselves of our professional services, a condition that continued with increasing regularity throughout our prisoner of war life."

Rumors proved to be the staff of life in these early days, providing some hope and the possibility of an end to the prisoners' humiliating plight. Many Filipinos gave what support they could. Prisoner Ben Waldron remembered marching down Dewey Boulevard and seeing the "V" for victory sign flashed by people lining the street; that stimulated him and many of his companions to hold their heads a bit higher and march more proudly in step.

The first word that Smith's family received in Sandwich came in a May 29 telegram: "The Navy Department regrets exceedingly to advise you that information has been received indicating that your husband Lieutenant Stanley Westbrook Smith Dental Corps United States Navy was performing his duty in the service of his country in the vicinity of Manila at the time it was captured about December 26. . . . No report of his death or injury has been received and he may be a Prisoner of War." Stanley Smith would be carried on naval records as "missing pending further information."

### THE RISING SUN APPEARS ON TAFT
### BOULEVARD — WE ARE POWs

They arrived on the evening of New Year's Day — down Taft and Dewey boulevards in trucks, cars, and military vehicles of all kinds bristling with armament, filled with troops with scowling faces and fixed bayonets. The Japanese civilians who had been interned in a detention camp across the street from us were heard shouting welcoming banzais and in general entering into an understandably wild celebration. We looked on in silent dejection from the windows at Scholastica; we were not pleased with what we saw.

However, we were relieved to note the troops' entrance appeared to be well organized and relatively subdued for what to them must have represented a momentous occasion. Armed guards appeared outside our hospital during the night, the gates of the wall surrounding it were closed to us, and Japanese signs were posted. Under death penalty we were not to destroy or mutilate any property — all had now become a part of the Imperial Japanese Empire. We anxiously awaited the arrival of someone in command for an indication of their plans for us.

Two high-ranking Japanese army officers arrived about 11:00 A.M. the following morning. Well guarded, they entered the compound to meet Captain Davis and Capt. Lyle Roberts for what they termed an interview regarding the incredible circumstances surrounding our being discovered there. They were not about to be convinced of our good intentions in remaining inside Manila when an avenue of escape so obviously remained open to us. They were adamant that such a situation was difficult for them to comprehend without suspicion. Was it any wonder?

For the time being we would be allowed to remain there as POWs through the magnanimity of the Japanese emperor, so we were told. We were given what appeared, under existing circumstances, an unnecessary order to stay within the confines of the Scholastica grounds; our final disposition would be decided later. We went about organizing our affairs as unobtrusively as we could, avoiding contact whenever possible with the uniformed armed guards, who began a day-and-night scheduled shuffle in and out of every nook and corner of the compound in their hobnailed boots.

We hadn't been indoctrinated with the required oriental bow (from the waist) whenever we met any of the military, so it wasn't long until slapping incidents occurred, which we eventually schooled ourselves to expect. This custom of slapping as a form of minor punishment could be compared to a tongue-lashing in our society: like, yet different, I can assure you. Slowly we began to learn by trial and error how to cope with these soldiers, who very cautiously went about their business of guarding us with ominous determination. They always traveled in pairs with fixed bayonets; even after diligent searching, they, too, couldn't believe we were unarmed and didn't have some ulterior military objective in mind. But as the days went by and we were not molested severely, our initial fears subsided.

During various stages of contradiction by one of their military groups and evasion or double-talk by another that might appear, almost everything was taken from us. We had managed to cache considerable food, drugs, clothing, and medical equipment sufficient to last us indefinitely. By gradual attrition these were removed by either Japanese army or navy, whichever was first to see something of value that appealed to them on their numerous inspections. Our microscopes particularly took their eye; they whisked them away early, and soon most of our drug and food supply was demanded. We voluntarily cut our meals to two light ones per day. Their policy was one of deprivation. First to go were the few liberties to which we felt entitled, then the material things they considered not essential to their interpretation of our well-being. We had yet to be subjected to the rice diet.

Almost daily a new restriction would be imposed, a new demand made, and some concession granted earlier, rescinded. Their whole philosophy centered on keeping us in a constant state of uncertainty and insecurity. Over and over again they cautioned us we were not to smile, to laugh, sing, or whistle; we could not show any animation, for we were a defeated people. They reminded us our navy had been sunk at Pearl Harbor, then would later tell us it was now being defeated in the Coral Sea and other South Pacific battles. It took us a while to appreciate how utterly determined they were to instill in us the conviction we were losing the war.

We had three sources of news, each one more or less distorted, in our opinion. The Japanese-controlled Manila press was still being published in English, but now, of course, with what we considered rank propaganda. Looking back, however, their successes were still so phenomenal that fabrication was quite unnecessary. Our next source of news was contact with the Japanese officers and enlisted men, some of whom had a fair command of English and were not inhibited in telling us how badly our forces were faring. They delighted in repeating the cliche that the war would last at least ten years and Japan was prepared to fight one hundred years. None of us, this early in our imprisonment, were influenced by such exaggeration, but it was difficult on occasion to overcome depressing reactions to their needling, which was their objective.

Our third source for current information was the Filipinos, upon whom we hopefully relied for what encouragement there might be. Loyally committed to brightening our horizon with good news, the Filipinos would smuggle in all manner of wild rumors: relief ships with men and ammunition were landing at Corregidor; MacArthur was counterattacking at the very gates of Manila and had released the report he would eat breakfast at the Manila Hotel on the morning of January 30. Many other choice tidbits perhaps were prompted by the sound of heavy gunfire in the distance. Throughout each day, in the general direction of Manila Bay, we could hear the sound of an artillery engagement, which we rationalized would be MacArthur's drive up Bataan Peninsula to retake Manila. From day to day we tried to estimate how much nearer they were than the day before, hopeful each night upon retiring that tomorrow would find them at the gates of our walled enclosure.

However, January 30 arrived and departed uneventfully. So we eagerly awaited the next current rumor the Filipinos might somehow smuggle in to us, and we never seemed to lose faith that the next one would contain some element of truth, and our spirits were continually nourished upon such fantasy provided by our friends.

As time slowly moved on and the Japanese reported such events as the sinking of the USS *Houston*, the fall of Singapore, and our reverses in Indonesia, we weren't so quick to discredit these reports as propaganda. The newspaper account of the *Houston* we could accept because of the very detailed description of its sinking and the bravery of the crew that went down, so they said, with all remaining guns blazing. The Japanese could afford to pay tribute to the enemy in those days. It was difficult to realize the fall of Singapore was as inevitable as the biased press had predicted, but, of course, we were learning to adjust to many discouraging situations we had not so long ago thought unlikely. In any event, we were now more concerned with the hope our government would never allow Corregidor to surrender for lack of reinforcement.

We were sometimes guilty of being unrealistically optimistic. One night, after extremely heavy gunfire was heard in the distance, our medical officer in charge cautioned the corpsmen, on watch now being maintained inside the compound throughout the night, to alert him when MacArthur's troops came down Taft Boulevard and to be sure to gather up the guns the guards at the front gate would probably throw away.

Again in March we were hopeful the counteroffensive was underway. One night, after we had secured the lights in the wards and were sitting on the steps outside enjoying the fresh air and star-filled sky, we became aware of two fast aircraft flying low over the general area of Nichols Airfield. Their running lights indicated intention to land, and we didn't consider it important until there were several loud explosions, and then antiaircraft fire was heard. Considerable commotion developed outside the wall and the Japanese guards came in brandishing their guns, waving everyone into the buildings. Elated, we retired with confidence the push was on and increased action tomorrow would certainly assure us liberation within a few days.

The next morning we received the guards' propaganda report on the activity of the previous night: two American planes had bombed Santo Tomas School, killing civilians. Later we learned from Filipinos how two U.S. planes from Corregidor had come in over Nichols with blinking lights, deceiving the Japanese, who proceeded to light the runways for what they presumed would be a landing of their Zero fighter aircraft. The lighted target was what our pilots hoped they would mistakenly provide them. The effect of such morale-boosting episodes usually lasted for days, but the infrequency of their occurrence was frustrating, and, of course, any real military significance negligible.

Another example of untoward optimism occurred when one of the doctors, as officer of the day, was sent to the front gate, inviting the guards, in the event of further bombing at night, to come inside the building to comparative safety with us. The doctor reluctantly carried out the order from his superior and got his face worked over for what the guards naturally considered an affront to their bravery. We eventually refrained from trying to "protect" the Japanese soldier and in so doing grew in stature and finesse as POWs.

We would climb the stairs in the early evening to an observation tower at Scholastica to get a panoramic view over Manila and distant Corregidor, confident now the heavy firing we had been hearing signaled the guns on Corregidor and Bataan devastating the Japanese positions. Occasionally big searchlights on the Rock could be seen scanning the bay, and we envisioned enemy boats blown out of the water. Manila was observing a blackout every night, and with the absence of practically all motorized traffic, the deathly stillness was made more phantomlike by smoldering fires periodically flaring up throughout the city, presenting a most eerie sight.

Filipino civilians neglecting to bow before the guards as they passed the front gates were severely beaten if they were caught. The poor Filipinos, like ourselves, were slow to grasp the realization that privileges offered in a democracy, so often taken for granted, can suddenly be swept away. It was a demoralizing blow; some POWs never did properly adjust to the reality of our predicament, and for the most part they were the ones who first succumbed to the inevitable hardships confronting us in the years ahead.

Our patients improved daily; many of the battle casualties were ready for duty but would not be available to our forces in Bataan and Corregidor. Our staff included approximately one hundred navy hospital corpsmen — valuable men whose services to the military in the field perhaps would have been crucial. Nearly thirty other personnel, including medical and dental officers, were POWs whose professional services here contributed little to the defense of the Philippines. Under circumstances so hopelessly beyond our control, it appeared that our careers had been needlessly sacrificed.

Confined so closely under such trying and tense circumstances, relationships soon became strained, and consideration for another person's viewpoint sometimes all but disappeared. One had to learn to ease out of a group discussion as it developed into an argument. It was too early to expect congenial adjustment in personalities under our forced incarceration.

The sisters had considerable tropical vegetation growing throughout the grounds, which I learned to appreciate more fully. There were bananas, hemp, coffee, and tea in addition to several mango and papaya trees. We also discovered the pomelo, a citrus fruit similar to our grapefruit but not nearly as good. It is apparently native to China and produced quite extensively there. At first we were only curiously interested; later on, tropical fruit, when available, became a very valuable supplement to our meager diet. Mangoes and papayas are a real delicacy anytime, anywhere.

### THE JAPANESE INTRODUCE THEIR POW POLICY

In February some officers of the Imperial Army, at the time in command of our group, appeared, informing us of a projected move the following week to a new, fully equipped hospital established by the Japanese. They would not disclose the location but instructed Captain Davis to select three doctors, one dentist, and sufficient corpsmen to help care for the sixty patients who would also be designated as part of the draft. Davis did his best to persuade them to keep our unit intact but received only stoical indifference, a frustration we would continue to experience in all our dealings with the Japanese in the days ahead. Thus began the unfolding of their policy of deception, which was to become a familiar pattern throughout our imprisonment; whenever we moved to a new location, they advised not taking anything with us — everything we needed would be provided in the new and much more desirable facility. Upon arrival we always encountered more austere surroundings, less food, and greater privation, including nonexistent medical provisions and more severe restrictions on all our activities. Our officers would ask for volunteers, but no one ever complied, perhaps from the old navy tradition of never volunteering for any type of duty. I suspect, more realistically, we held back not because of any existing comforts we enjoyed in our present location but rather from the uncertainty of what additional hardship the change was certain to bring.

We hadn't sufficiently recovered from the initial emotional disturbance experienced in becoming military prisoners of war. Our reaction at the time was to retain, at all costs, we thought, whatever security could be derived from association with each other as a unit; separation aroused serious forebodings, a fear of something like disappearing into a void. On the appointed day the front gate closed upon our fellow prisoners, and nothing was heard of their whereabouts for many weeks.

Then one day we were pleasantly surprised and greatly relieved to have Dr. Lambert, a medical officer in the departed group, brought in under guard, accompanying a former patient who had been injured on a work detail. Dr. Lambert wisely used the occasion to request the patient be brought to Scholastica, where equipment was available for X-rays. It also gave him an opportunity to inform us about the welfare of the group. Although closely observed, he was able, in guarded tones, to tell us they had been taken to Pasay Elementary School in the Paranaque district and interned under the most severe conditions.

We considered the matter gravely. Becoming more convinced each day of their determination to deny us the reasonable comforts of Scholastica as well as to separate us from any association with civilians (offered here through occasional contact with the sisters in a separate building), we had reason to be apprehensive.

Exactly one month to the day, we were ordered to have another draft of patients and staff standing by — with the same propaganda about going to a fully equipped and, as they reported it, "more better" hospital. Not many believed it this time, although Davis and Roberts, his assistant, appeared to. Roberts admonished us not to take any food, drugs, clothing, or other supplies stored at Scholastica; everything we had, he said, was no longer ours. It all belonged to the Japanese.

Dr. Erickson, the physician selected for this move, requested I be the group's dental officer, who would accompany him. Dr. Cross, our erratic senior dental officer (a real friend), provided me with many useful articles he proceeded to scrounge up from the supplies we had been cautioned *not* to take. In fact, before I left he had filled my duffel bag to its capacity, and I was most thankful.

I admit I was less than enthusiastic about moving but resigned myself to the inevitable. Each time a move was required we became more proficient in concealing from the guards, who always made a thorough inspection of our possessions before leaving, the things we suspected they would take from us. It became quite a game of sorts, and we more often than not won. They found a gun in the luggage of a navy line officer patient in our group; astounding his fellow shipmates, you can imagine the stir it created among the guards who uncovered it. Baltzley was quite a character; as a POW patient he was to give us many trying moments in the months and years ahead. As we were leaving, the Japanese told us we would join the first group at Pasay; somehow it eased the situation greatly — we would be glad to see them.

The ride from Scholastica, during which we were exposed to view in Japanese military trucks under armed guard, produced mixed feelings in all of us. For the first time we were paraded as prisoners before our Philippine friends, and we were apprehensive about how they would react. The Filipinos along the way, however, only occasionally glanced our way as some brave soul would hastily give us a furtive "V" for victory sign before turning away.

Many Filipinos openly defied the invading forces during the early days of occupation, and at first the Japanese were somewhat restrained in their attempts to win their cooperation. Passive resistance of the civilian population, nevertheless, was to become increasingly more stubborn throughout the war, and as time went on the approach used by the military became less subtle. The Japanese objective in submitting American prisoners to humiliation before the Filipinos was to undermine the confidence they had built up in us. I am sure they didn't completely fail in their attempt.

It was obvious the Japanese were totally unprepared, and perhaps understandably so, to establish prisoner-of-war facilities when they arrived in Manila, but it is difficult to explain their selection of the little elementary school at Pasay as a place of confinement. The most plausible explanation, I suspect, was simply a matter of expediency. Upon arrival we were told to leave our duffel bags on the school doorstep as we climbed from the truck and were shoved inside the building by the guards. We looked through a window to the interior, where we saw machine guns in position facing the enclosed yard beyond, a small area measuring perhaps seventy-five by one hundred feet.

As we entered the building we were confronted with a tough-looking, battle-scarred sergeant whose staff around him gave every indication of being equally as tough. There was little ceremony, after a very thorough shakedown, in directing us through a small opening in a barbed-wire fence, bringing us for the first time in contact with our former shipmates who had arrived some weeks earlier. We were relieved to see their familiar faces but depressed with what we surveyed otherwise.

It didn't take long to learn what we could expect at Pasay. Its physical arrangement included some twenty one-story small rooms, barren of equipment, enclosing the four sides of the yard. For the duration of our stay there, we would sit and sleep on the floor, as all furniture had been removed. The rooms in the back and on the sides of the encircled yard opened onto a narrow continuous porch that faced the square enclosure in the middle. What had been the school's offices, located in front and forming the fourth side of the enclosure, were taken over by the guards. They were separated from the prisoners by the barbed-wire fence and the mounted machine guns we had observed upon arrival.

All outside windows within the rooms were covered with heavy boards. The barbed wire, literally as well as figuratively, was being drawn closer and closer around us; we were prisoners in every sense of the word. Any doubt remaining was quickly dispelled when we were served our first rice meal that evening. This was a special occasion, for we were served an added delicacy: a soup made from a few slightly tainted fish boiled in water, unsalted. I wasn't that hungry — yet.

The following morning we spent evaluating our new surroundings. Not the least depressing aspect of the whole situation was our supper of the night before, the first food the occupation forces had provided. POWs from now on had to prepare their own chow, and to a degree some crude provisions were made for it. Equipment was limited to large iron cauldrons (fifty-gallon pots, or callas). They had issued two for cooking all food provided to the camp: rice and occasionally some other item such as edible weeds for making an insipid mess referred to as soup and, rarely, small sardine-size fish we boiled whole. All cooking was done over an open fire in the yard.

Our navy corpsmen assigned to the cook's detail soon became proficient in preparing rice in these open pits. A thin crust would generally brown and adhere to the sides of the callas; this crust was later removed and fed to especially undernourished POWs as extra food. We all soon acquired a taste for rice and consumed it to the last kernel in our mess kits. On rare occasions when some Philippine raw sugar became available through devious means, it made a delightful addition to our rice menu.

Sleeping on the floor was a new POW experience for us. For the most part we were allowed to keep the contents of our duffel bags, after rigid inspection, and those of us who had blankets and a mosquito net were fortunate. We removed some blackboards from the walls, pulling nails from wherever we could to improvise a raised platform about six inches off the floor. The composition material provided much more comfort than the hard floor for sleeping, or so we thought. Surprisingly we soon adjusted to this makeshift platform. The guards, strangely enough, didn't interfere with our plundering things to meet our needs; destruction of certain parts of the rooms did not appear to disturb them at all, and we apparently never went beyond the limits of their curiosity to observe what we were up to.

The Japanese very early in the war became aware of the clever resourcefulness of the average American GI, and soon they were relying upon the ingenious nature of the enlisted POW to fabricate all manner of things for their convenience. Either this wasn't a gift of their own troops, or more likely it suited their fancy to have American prisoners subservient to them. Material return for such services generally amounted to additional rice not eaten from the guard's mess kits or perhaps access to a few cigarettes. Later on, as the GI became enlightened to the full potentialities of his position, he was able on countless occasions to reap fabulous returns from this relationship — benefits many times accruing to the whole camp. It didn't take the astute GI prisoner long to capitalize on every opportunity, sometimes at great risk to himself.

Pasay was under the military supervision of Lieutenant Kusomoto, who made periodic inspections of the front office guards, occasionally sauntering through to inspect us. At such times he would enter into conversation with Dr. Brokenshire, a naval reserve officer who was presently the senior physician at Pasay. Before being called to active duty, "Broke" had been a medical missionary in Davao. Kusomoto was one of the better Japanese officers with whom we would come in contact. He could speak and understand English with little effort.

It was the camp sergeant, nevertheless, as far as our daily contacts were concerned, who had complete control over us. The particular diversion of the joker in charge of us now was to get rip-roaring drunk about three nights a week, timing the episodes when he least expected Kusomoto would appear. On these occasions we would make ourselves as inconspicuous as possible by staying close to our rooms, trying to ignore all the shouting and noise he created throwing chairs and tables against the bulkhead in his office. Frayed nerves, fortunately, were all we ever really suffered as a result of his hilarious activity; however, with those machine guns directed at us we were never sure what bent the sergeant's private brawl might take. He was an emotionally disturbed individual all right, perhaps suffering from battle fatigue, the drunken bouts possibly his escape from reality.

### A CRUDE ATTEMPT AT BRAINWASHING

One inspection made at Pasay I shall never forget. On this particular day we were warned to have our area of the compound in proper order for the visit of a high-ranking officer who would appear. We knew by the usual explosive shout of the guards heralding such dignitaries when Kusomoto and this officer arrived at the front office. We were all herded into the yard at attention, ready to bow when the party came into the enclosed area. In appearance and performance the visiting colonel would have been exceptionally well chosen as lead in a Gilbert and Sullivan comic opera, from his bartender's mustache down to his baggy trousers, ill-fitting boots, and long, dangling sword that seemed to rival him in height. The corpsmen appropriately dubbed him "Whiskers." He was here, so he said, to inform us of our sorry plight. In halting English he read the Imperial Rescript of the Emperor declaring war against the enemy. We learned later it was read to the Japanese troops by the military throughout the war on certain days set aside for that purpose. It served to spark any lagging enthusiasm the soldier in the ranks might be experiencing, and the psychology of it worked very well. For several days thereafter we would feel the impact of its message through the rigid attitude of the guards toward us.

The colonel's propaganda efforts were most fantastic, and more amusing than convincing. Did we know, for instance, his country's troops had now overrun everything in the Far East all the way to Australia? His assistants displayed maps on which the flags of the Rising Sun were in evidence to substantiate his statement. Every island in the Pacific was now in possession of the Japanese. For our special benefit he displayed a large photograph, which we suspected was a bit of trick photography, showing the destruction of our fleet at Pearl Harbor and other extensive damage at Hawaii. He would frequently pause to swagger, lean on his samurai sword, and shout, "What do you think of your future now?" Well, we knew what we thought all right, but we gave him the old fish-eye silent treatment.

Because we apparently did not respond as he had anticipated, or at least to his satisfaction, he finally stomped off the porch and back into the front office muttering to himself in Nipponese. We rated him with a big "E" for effort, never really knowing what response he actually expected to this tirade, but I will confess the tension eased greatly when he made his exit. Fortunately we did not encounter him again; however, many other POWs were to come under his arrogant tactics as camp commander at O'Donnel, San Fernando, where the Bataan Death March was to terminate.

One other early confrontation resulting from prison routine proved most interesting. During our early imprisonment at Pasay each of us was summoned to the front office for interrogation by a Japanese civilian interpreter. Horai, dressed partly in military khaki, spoke in a hoarse, rasping voice probably indicating a bronchial condition either alcoholic or tubercular in origin. This handicap, together with his limited English vocabulary, presented us some difficulty in following him as he compiled his information. The Japanese military also attach great significance to their paperwork, so we became subjects of endless questioning by them at various times as POWs. They labored long hours with pencil and ink brush compiling statistics — no doubt promptly filed and forgotten according to usual military procedure.

This interpreter, in his harmless way, wanted to encourage us, I believe, so at some time during the interview he would say to each of us, "Soon you go home to family; you wife-u?" If we brightened at this bit of optimistic outlook he would follow with, "You son?" Typical of many cultures, his primary interest was in the male progeny. We discovered he had been a civilian vegetable merchant at Baguio before the war, but he proved too inadequate, and Horai was finally removed as interpreter after a few drunken escapades.

Through printed material they circulated, together with pressure brought to bear on numerous occasions, we were convinced we should have a working knowledge of Japanese; *Nippon-go* was their term for it. One day we were perfunctorily informed that *tenko*, in Japanese, would be held both morning and evening. Tenko was military muster, or quarters, as we in the navy would call it. We assembled in the yard at the designated time, where at the shout of *"bango"* (count off) by the guard on duty, we would begin: *Ichi, ni, san, shi, go, roku, shichi, hachi, ku, ju;* then *ju-ichi* for eleven and so on.

Unpleasant experiences, cropping up with greater frequency, persuaded us we shouldn't delay further in acquiring a much broader understanding of their language than being able to count off; many of the Japanese soldiers couldn't or wouldn't speak English. To protect our well-being it was important at least to be able to comprehend what might be an order with an "or else" implied or otherwise stated. It became diplomatically convenient to greet our "benefactors" with an *ahayoo* to wish them a good morning, or in the afternoon a pleasant *konnichi wa,* and later on we might venture a *konban wa,* or good evening. Some POWs became quite proficient in speaking and understanding Nipponese, but all of us began to view the subject more objectively.

The Japanese never gave a command in a tone other than a guttural shout. When they brought their military or us peons to attention (*kiotsuke*), it would come out more nearly as a loud belch from deep inside. It seemed to us the smallest in stature produced the more stentorian tone, as if he were determined to compensate somehow. In many respects this served a useful purpose, for we were always forewarned when the arrival of some ranking officer who might inspect us was given military recognition by the guard shack out front.

The endless monotony of our restricted routine was such that describing the passage of time with the expression snail's pace would be a gross understatement. In the evening, after rice, a horrible Japanese substitute for soup, and tenko, we would sit in the congested enclosed schoolyard watching the sun go down behind the front office.

We derived some satisfaction by referring to it as the Nipponese Rising Sun, soon to be eclipsed. Reminiscing about things dear to us, passing along the various rumors the outside work details would bring in at night from the Filipinos, hopefully anticipating our release in the near future; thus we would manage to spend the evening until it was time to retire to our mosquito nets and fabricated beds on the floor of the little schoolrooms.

One wild rumor I recall during this period told of Japan's being bombed daily — so severely that Nippon had asked for a temporary cessation of hostilities to bury her dead. A morale booster like that really cheered us; no doubt it was the Filipinos' colorful exaggeration of Doolittle's token raid over the city of Tokyo. We projected three years too early a Japan being brought to submission with carpet bombing; however, this conjured vision did a lot to lift our spirits at the time.

Increasing air activity shattered any optimism we had been sharing about early liberation. Medium and heavy Japanese bombers were taking off and landing from nearby Nichols almost continuously during the days just before Bataan and Corregidor fell. It was impossible, of course, to estimate the success of their missions; however, the faithful Filipinos had smuggled in word reporting 70 percent of the planes being shot down over Corregidor, a most gratifying, though groundless, rumor.

Old "Pop" Seal, the "Bamboo" American (term for an American living in the Philippines for a long time) who for (too) many years had been on active duty with our 31st Infantry stationed in Intramuros, was the handyman around camp who collected the rumors. His mestizo wife and children were living nearby, so friends and family contacted him almost daily at our back fence or in the alley where he would often be doing odd jobs for the guards. They reported the latest news developments in Tagalog, the native tongue. Assuming the Filipinos passing by were innocent of any mischief, the guards little suspected what a valuable packet of current information was being peddled in Pop's direction to be parceled on to us (probably with embellishment). His evening rumor session was generally the bright spot of the day, but it was not very often in accordance with actual world events.

The high point of our internment at Pasay came when three of us were allowed to visit a nearby Philippine open market to purchase native food. First we had to convince Yamashita, a new sergeant, that it was in the best interests of the camp. This was not too difficult, for he appeared to have a more humanitarian view regarding our needs. On occasion he would even invite some of us into his office to talk about any subject except the war. So we pooled our resources and went "ashore" one day to the Paranaque market, with the sergeant attired in his best uniform and sword. We had the freedom of the place while Yamashita wandered about relishing the atmosphere he created with his American prisoners of war.

In addition to the merchandise the Filipinos insisted upon our taking without charge, we managed to purchase a one-hundred-pound sack of raw peanuts and one of mongo beans. We also bought all the bananas and *calimensies* (small limes) one little calesa pony was able to haul back into camp. We resold everything in small quantities to patients and staff, thereby recovering our peso investment. This venture had a tremendous impact on the camp and provided vital supplement to our meager diet. Yamashita wisely warned us against exposing any of the produce whenever inspection parties came through; however, we were already becoming adept at always hiding things from the Japanese. He was the kindest sergeant we ever encountered.

### OUR WALLS BEGIN TO CRUMBLE

One night we suddenly awakened to a violent upheaval all around us. The walls, the ceiling, the floor, everything was creaking and straining as if someone were shaking the whole building and earth beneath. It didn't last long, but most prisoners hurried out into the yard in the excitement, only to be shouted back by the guards. This was our first encounter with a Philippine earthquake, and sleeping on the floor we got the full impact of its eeriness.

The next morning Yamashita told us Bataan had surrendered, and he was being transferred to Tarlac to help handle the forty-some-thousand prisoners who were arriving from Bataan. The announcement was a severe blow to our weakening morale, but we hung on to the hope that Corregidor would not surrender. Hearts were heavy in Pasay on that day, April 9, 1942.

After the fall of Bataan, we observed for the first time a tone of bitterness creeping into conversations among personnel. Four months without any evidence of reinforcements, either naval or air, for the beleaguered Philippine garrisons brought us to the realization that in all probability none would be arriving in the near future. It was most difficult for us to understand why the Allied Front had not responded to the desperate situation developing in the Philippines. As a result, discouragement and despair, undermining what had been a reasonably healthy mental outlook on the part of almost all POWs, began to have a hearing in camp.

Shortly after Bataan had capitulated, we witnessed the last U.S. plane engaged in any type of aggressive action against the enemy until we observed Allied air strikes directed at Japan prior to her collapse in 1945. A high-flying reconnaissance aircraft made a run over Manila, successfully dropping a few bombs on a motor pool target. It appeared to us at the time as a feeble and desperate finale, for we were hearing rumors of the imminent fall of Corregidor now. Japanese artillery were pounding our defenses from Bataan Peninsula positions denied them until recently.

Finally in May, before Corregidor surrendered, Captain Davis and our remaining POW friends were brought to Pasay. When the Japanese recovered sufficiently from the initial surprise of finding us in Manila, I am confident they made plans to remove all of us from Scholastica as soon as it could be arranged. Scholastica had been a source of irritation to them from the beginning. They surmised we had hopes of being left there for the duration of the war, and the relative comforts we had provided were not tolerated by the Japanese in a place of confinement for prisoners of war. We also felt they had greedy thoughts about the substantial quantities of medical and food supplies we had cached there. This move of the Davis stragglers, the remaining personnel at Scholastica, accomplished their objective.

Survivors of the infamous Bataan Death March, often described as a carnival of sadism, were soon being brought to Pasay by the Japanese from various work details they had established in and around Manila. Although physically incapacitated these lads would volunteer for anything, hopeful of a chance to escape the treatment they were receiving at the prison stockade in San Fernando. Their near-starvation diet during the latter phases of the Bataan Campaign, when food and communication to the lines all but disappeared, had already taken its toll. The hardships experienced in the death march, with starvation levels imposed this time by the Nipponese, soon brought them to a state of complete physical exhaustion.

The strenuous manual labor the Japanese demanded was out of the question for these poor fellows, and at the point of collapse they were brought to POW areas of concentration for whatever treatment might be available. This practice was to continue throughout the war. Except for malaria cases the only care generally indicated involved a well-balanced diet — in quantities and kind not provided. Until the signing of the peace terms in Tokyo, inadequate food was to remain one of the greatest determining factors in POW survival.

In early May, Captain Hoeffel, the commander of naval forces on Corregidor, joined us at Pasay, confirming the rumor we had heard of the surrender. His party, after wading ashore, had been marched from a nearby beach where they had disembarked from cattle boats bringing them from the Rock. There were several high-ranking officers in the group, including General King and Lieutenant Commander McCoy, the navy communication officer who would later make his escape at Mindanao through Filipino guerrilla assistance. They were a bedraggled lot, physically and emotionally exhausted.

We now experienced a population explosion at Pasay as we tried to accommodate some six hundred prisoners on a twenty-four-hour basis in a space and with sanitary facilities planned to supply the needs of perhaps two hundred children during a school day. Our limited plumbing was continually becoming clogged with the heavy demands made upon it; our open garbage pit was rapidly developing into a fly-infested cesspool. Only a hot tropical sun spared us from an epidemic nurtured in such unhygienic, terribly overcrowded surroundings. Apparently the Japanese, too, were beginning to realize, even under their questionable standards, that Pasay Elementary School had outlived its usefulness as a detention camp for war prisoners.

Chapter 3

# What Is Our Quan Having This Evening?

Bilibid Prison, where Smith was transferred on May 30, 1942, was formerly a Spanish and later an American prison. Its massive stone and cement walls became a familiar sight to nearly all American captives from the Philippine campaign. United States authorities had held Japanese civilians there until Manila was abandoned, and the Japanese now reciprocated, first confining medical and other personnel captured in and around the open city. Bilibid became known to the Japanese as "the hospital," according to Dr. Thomas Hayes, whose stay at the prison overlapped Smith's.

On July 1, Comdr. Lee B. Sartin (medical corps, USN), American camp commander, appointed Smith to organize, construct, and operate a special diet galley to cook extra food for the malnourished and gravely ill patients. Three corpsmen assigned to work with him assisted in preparing food for an average of one hundred patients a day. They were aided by a courageous civilian, a former school teacher from Manila known only as Mrs. Norton, who secured large quantities of extra food to supplement the special diet.

This operation continued successfully until the fall of 1943, when outside supplies began to dwindle (Mrs. Norton was finally refused permission to bring in additional food), and as Smith wrote, "Japanese indifference to our welfare increased." Stanley Smith left Bilibid on October 2, 1943, ordered to be taken to Cabanatuan POW camp.

The Japanese attitude toward prisoners of war needs to be understood, because it plays a major role in the story. As Saburo Ienaga wrote in his book *The Pacific War*, the Japanese code of war was not to withdraw or surrender and "not [to] be taken prisoner alive." They were at first overwhelmed and unprepared when the Americans surrendered their entire Philippine force, plus civilian internees. It was not until March 1942 that the surprised Japanese war ministry had even established the Prisoner of War Administration Division. By the end of the year an estimated 20,200 Americans were in prison camps, more than 13,000 in the Philippines alone.

Brutality was a way of life for the Japanese soldier, John Toland concluded in his book *The Rising Sun,* and the soldier in turn beat and slapped those under his authority. When prisoners failed to comprehend orders or were too weak to follow them, the frustrated captors often reacted violently. Of course, there were those sadistic camp guards who actually enjoyed mistreating prisoners; one American POW after another testified to that.

Several of the people mentioned in this narrative also appear in other accounts. The Japanese Dr. Nogi was credited by Ben Waldron in *Corregidor, "From Paradise to Hell"* as being "the first and ONLY Japanese I had encountered who was decent to me while I was a prisoner of war." Hayes also liked him, as he did Sartin, describing Nogi as an "honest, sympathetic soul of kindness and fair play."

Hayes, who did not survive the war, accused the Japanese, in his posthumously published *Bilibid Diary,* of allowing American prisoners to die in order to surpass the number of Japanese deaths during the Bataan campaign: "There is a feeling that this is not coincidental, but according to plan" (Hayes, 27). He also believed that prisoners were placed near every probable military objective on Luzon (for example, the Americans transferred to Japan in 1942 to work in factories) to cleverly advertise the "fact that we would be bombing our own people" (Hayes, 111).

Back in Sandwich anxious family and friends waited nearly a year before word was finally received about the fate of Stanley Smith. The navy, after hearing from official Japanese sources via Geneva, notified his wife on May 4, 1943, that he was "now a prisoner of war." The letter concluded, "The Secretary of the Navy appreciates your anxiety and directs me to inform you that the Department of State is making every effort to assure the welfare of prisoners of war." Several more months passed before the first heavily censored POW postcard arrived on August 13, the same day word came from the War Department that a package (limited to eleven pounds) could be sent via the Red Cross.

This was followed by a second postcard on September 4, which mentioned Freeland Corners, a rural site near where Ila Smith had grown up. That, as the Sandwich *Free Press* noted September 8, assured her that the "message was really sent by him."

WE PREPARE TO MOVE AGAIN — BILIBID

R anking field officers were to be transferred to a more favorable camp — so those at Pasay were notified. At the time, it did appear logical for these older men to be given preferential treatment, and it was also apparent to the rest of us that the officers we knew heartily approved of the idea, with little evidence of disappointment at the thought of leaving us. Like so many misconceptions harbored in those days, it turned out the Japanese were using this occasion to separate the "gold braid" from hoi polloi. The officers eventually found themselves again in similar short-rationed, rigidly policed, unsanitary concentration areas — Formosa and later Korea, where menial labor in camp was also expected of them. Indeed, it was demanded for their survival.

Someone of navy rank had to remain in command of our original hospital group, and Dr. L. B. Sartin (Commander) was so designated when the rest of the senior officers were taken from Pasay. The guards circulated a rumor we also would be moved, probably many, many kilometers away, north of Manila to a new camp. Informed we would be required to hike, carrying our gear, we began to streamline our possessions into one duffel bag supported on our backs.

We eventually were told to be ready May 30, and on Memorial Day we made the second in a series of moves that would confront almost all of us in the years immediately ahead. In accordance with the policy of uncertainty and confusion the Japanese had heretofore maintained, we were told while being loaded into army vehicles that we would find ourselves at Bilibid at the end of the route, not the destination they had originally hinted at. Feeling terribly depressed over the situation, we were again trucked through Manila streets now newly named and distinctly identified in Nipponese.

Bilibid, until the time of our arrival at the front gate, had remained something of an enigma to POWs. The mystery surrounding what was to be found inside this walled bastille had been a topic of conversation among POWs for many weeks; foreboding rumors had come to us that it was comparable to the worst facilities so far provided by the Japanese.

It had a long, sordid history, first as a Spanish prison, then a Filipino. However, prior to the war it had been abandoned because of its physical deterioration, and some of the buildings were in the process of being dismantled. The high stone walls, still intact, made it the logical center for prisoner concentration in Manila. Bilibid became a legend familiar to all those who fought the invasion of the Philippines in World War II and lived to experience its unwholesome environment.

Thousands of American army and navy prisoners had passed through Bilibid since the fall of Corregidor. The buildings were so crowded with sick GIs on the floors that hundreds of others had to sleep on the ground outside wherever they could find space. Many prisoners were too sick and weak from dysentery to move very far from the spot where they wearily dropped what was left of their luggage upon arrival. Sufficient toilet facilities to care for their needs did not exist; refuse and excreta of all descriptions were to be found everywhere, creating a terrific stench. Much of the diarrhea so prevalent was transmitted by the mass of flies swarming undisturbed over everything.

Guards were about as numerous as the flies; they seemed to be everywhere. Until now, we had encountered them for the most part only at the front gates. Apparently these small brown-skinned privates had been recently transferred from the hard-fought campaign at Bataan and Corregidor, a battle-crusted lot having little if any sympathy and still less regard for their recent adversaries. Although outwardly expressionless, they received immense satisfaction, I suspect, from observing our humility in having to bow from the waist whenever confronting one of them. This custom, so strange to us, has always existed in Japan; it is their way of showing respect to superiors, and there was no question now in our minds (or theirs) who was exercising authority.

We were all disheartened with what we saw. The whole situation, as we first surveyed it, looked so discouraging as to appear almost hopeless for survival over any prolonged period of confinement. We had reached a new low during our first five months as POWs, and our future looked most uncertain. In the early days at Bilibid the military in charge appeared infrequently, and our appeals to their officers for medication and sufficient food went unheeded.

I surmise those responsible for what turned out to be a prolonged, costly, and frustrating Philippine campaign were still feeling the effects of the delay in success. You might say we were experiencing some of the backlash from the criticism the Japanese commanders most probably had received from imperial authority. As part of their problem, we, too, were made to suffer. Ignoring our needs was a penalty we would have to withstand.

The physical makeup of what was to constitute home for many of us for a long time to come couldn't have been more adroitly engineered for its intended purpose by the Japanese themselves. Cement cell blocks, like spokes in a wheel, radiated out in all directions from a central control tower now occupied by the guards on duty, making an ideal arrangement for maintaining constant vigil of all activities within the walled enclosure.

Aside from one or two trees and a blade of grass here and there, vegetation of any sort was practically nonexistent in Bilibid. Our only outlook was over a thirty-foot stone wall, affording little but a tropical sky to relieve the drabness within. Though not visible to us inside, the trotting sound the hoofs of the little ponies made pulling colorful two-wheeled calesas on Manila streets outside the wall, at the insistent urging of their drivers, was to remind us life went on out there regardless of our miserable confinement within. This didn't lessen the despair we felt over our predicament nor make the loneliness any less.

When the initial shock of finding things in such a lamentable state wore off, Dr. Sartin called his staff together to attack the problem with the materials at hand. Sanitation was our greatest concern and dysentery the most urgent medical problem, the two being directly related. With sick patients lying willy-nilly all over the compound, most of them weak and emaciated from diarrhea, malaria, and insufficient food, realistic control in such an environment was impossible. The first step was to thoroughly clean one of the buildings to accommodate and isolate the worst cases.

After certain buildings were designated as wards, a general scrubbing detail was established and a semblance of hospital organization and procedure put into operation. We obtained Japanese cooperation, in fact outspoken approval for what we were doing, until they were confronted with Dr. Sartin's urgent request to provide us ample diet in sufficient quantities and pertinent medication for the sick. Debate, evasion, and procrastination were the only fruits of our endeavor in that direction. We couldn't have had a better spokesman, however, than Dr. Sartin. He was patient yet persistent, tactful yet fearless in his dealings with the Japanese, qualities of judgment our experience so far taught us were essential for any measure of success.

Our contact with the Nipponese authorities at Bilibid was no different from what we had experienced as POWs so far and were to continue to encounter throughout the war. Proper sanitation, adequate food, and certain specific medications would have satisfactorily handled 95 percent of all frustrating problems eventually to develop in prisoners of war. The answer was so simple, the reason so obvious; yet the need for food and medicine continued, except on a few occasions, to be one of the most disturbing of all our confrontations with them. The Japanese could never be convinced. Their baffling answer always remained contrary: the sick prisoners needed less food, not more, for they were not doing any physical labor.

Dr. Nogi, the physician who inspected us at Bilibid, finally did bring us some charcoal as a gesture of responsibility in providing medication for our dysentery patients. A very high percentage of the worst cases died, although many more with stronger constitutions and a determined will to survive did pull through — not because of the charcoal provided us. In the definitive outcome, we observed over and over again how vitally important was the will to live on the part of the patient. So many lost hope, and when a depressing outlook was present in the patient in the absence of all other support, favorable chance of recovery remained questionable.

It wasn't long until evidence of beriberi was observed in the patients brought to Bilibid, and throughout the months ahead it was to become the predominating diagnosis. Inadequate food, particularly improper food balance, affected all prisoners at various times. The seriousness of the condition was relative, depending upon one's ability to adjust to a limited rice diet. The metabolism of some adjusted quite readily; others never adjusted sufficiently to prevent onset of serious deficiency symptoms. The doctors referred to it as a hypo-proteinemia syndrome with varying levels of bodily damage: not enough protein in the diet was the causative factor.

I recall one extreme case of beriberi in the "L" building who received all the extra food (protein) we were able to give him. He had been an outstanding high school athlete in his hometown, somewhere in Ohio. Extensive edema of advanced beriberi had now overextended his body tissues to the point where his physique lost all natural contour and tone, developing finally into something resembling a hideous, inflated caricature one might see in a street parade. His strength finally failed to the point that increasing weight of body fluids prevented him from standing, and before he died his eyeballs had a tendency to drop out of their sockets when he moved about.

There were many unpleasant things we encountered during those days at Bilibid, and he was only one of many who were lost when the ravages of beriberi finally reached the heart muscles of the maladjusted victim. It was an interesting disclosure that multiple doses of synthetic vitamins, which we occasionally obtained in Japan as the war was drawing to a close, never proved successful in treating these cases. However, in the few instances where sufficient protein in the diet could be included with the vitamins, all deficiency symptoms disappeared.

Our occupancy of the long, rectangular cement block buildings had to conform to a pattern. Having no partitions in them simplified assigning floor space on either of the long sides, leaving a passageway in the middle for traffic. We soon adjusted to sleeping, in spite of the disturbance the guards created throughout the night shuffling through the entire length of the building with their heavy hobnailed boots and flashing lights.

We became accustomed to the cement floor without beds. No doubt some of the war-weary Japanese invading troops in Manila at the time were trying, for the first time in their lives, to adapt to beds with mattress and springs that replaced the customary tatami floor mats used in Japan. Our adjustment was the more difficult, I am sure; we were informed that if a Japanese soldier had to endure hardship, so should we. Their opinion was in no danger of being openly challenged.

After we had succeeded in getting Bilibid to function on a more satisfactory basis, we were confronted with a major sanitation problem. Notwithstanding the inevitable demands the dysentery patients were making upon our toilet facilities, we would in any event have been called upon to fabricate some type of substitution for inadequate plumbing. A warrant officer POW came up with a practical solution similar to the Japanese *benjo* (toilet). A long wooden straddle-trench, wide enough but not so wide as to inhibit assuming the characteristic Philippine squat (sitting on your heels), was built out in the open air and sunshine. It was long enough to accommodate the hurried needs of twenty-five or more people at a time; reading material and toilet paper were not provided, however.

The ingenious aspect of the project was the simple engineering concept that periodically flushed the entire trough. Elevated at one end on a delicately balanced axis was a large scoop of approximately fifty gallons, scavenged somewhere (with Japanese assistance) and brought into the compound. Running water was allowed to fill this large receptacle until its weight finally overbalanced the scoop, causing it to empty the water into the trench, where a built-in grade flushed the contents of its entire length into the sewer at the lower end.

When emptied, the scoop was balanced to return to an upright position, ready to be refilled and again complete the self-flushing cycle. In this manner the flow of water was so controlled as to allow the benjo to be flushed about every twenty minutes. It was clean, sanitary, required little maintenance, served an urgent need, was well ventilated, and helped to eliminate any false modesty unconsciously buried deep inside those called upon to use it.

The food at Bilibid fell into a routine that would continue, with very few exceptions, for the duration. Variation in a diet planned exclusively around rice, prepared with the primitive equipment provided, taxed one's ingenuity almost to the point of no return. The time came, however, when a prisoner consumed his rice three times a day at mealtime with as much relish as he would have a steak at home; in fact, visualizing the steak sometimes helped us to enjoy the rice more completely.

The prevailing topic of conversation among POWs soon centered around food of all descriptions. A recipe including the richest of ingredients was always the most popular; the kind that would make you drool remained the most captivating of all. It became a favorite pastime for patients in an otherwise dreary environment.

Our cuisine was limited to rice prepared in one of two ways. For breakfast it would be prepared in the fifty-gallon callas over the usual pit fire as a watery gruel called *lugao* in the Philippines. A canteen cup was the usual ration. At all other times an attempt was made to steam the rice. Occasionally we would have access to some salt for seasoning, and, more often than we liked, our serving of rice included little, white, weevil-like worms and mice leavings for whatever weird seasoning they afforded. The rice furnished at the beginning of the occupation was very poor in quality. I would not be at all surprised if the Filipinos maliciously unloaded this old rice onto the Japanese authorities, and perhaps they in turn derived some satisfaction in passing it on to us; in any case we came out on the short end of the deal. It is amazing how the pangs of hunger can overcome fastidiousness, for we soon had no qualms about picking the foreign bodies from our lugao.

On rare occasions various amounts and kinds of fish were brought to the galley to be boiled into a gravy-like consistency, providing a welcome change in the diet and adding a flavor to the rice. There were other less frequent times when the fish would be large enough, ample enough in quantity, and not sufficiently spoiled to steam whole and serve a portion to each POW.

I recall the Japanese sending in the skeleton of a tuna fish I would estimate to have weighed about one hundred or so pounds. All the edible portion had been removed, leaving the bony skeleton resembling, more than anything else, a museum piece. Under any other circumstances it would have been amusing, but we were hungry and felt a mistake had been made. On the strength of such a possibility, Dr. Sartin showed the carcass to the Japanese quartermaster. It wasn't a mistake, we were told; it would make a delicious flavor for soup. We buried it.

Persistent effort to secure more nourishing food for the sick finally brought the first break in what had been until now a solid front of opposition and indifference to our problem. This was the beginning of a whole new approach, although of relatively short duration, to handling our deficient diet cases, and we were quick to seize the opportunity.

Apparently a considerable amount of canned evaporated milk remained in storage when Corregidor was overrun by the Japanese; I am confident it was but a fraction of the total loot they acquired at its fall. Dr. Nogi agreed to ration us about a case a day of this confiscated milk if we would provide means for and assurance that it would be distributed only to those who were sufficiently ill to warrant it. He also agreed to limited buying of additional food through outside Manila markets if the POWs could pay for it.

### THE BILIBID DIET KITCHEN

Dr. Sartin asked whether I would assume responsibility for a special diet kitchen to prepare and serve this extra food for the heavy sick, all of whom were beginning to show evidence of nutritional deficiency. We had practically no materials with which to work; however, two resourceful corpsmen were assigned to assist me in this detail. I was to act in liaison with the ward doctors in determining the patients who would qualify for this extra food we planned to prepare.

The two hospital corpsmen, Mayberry and Thompson (whom we called "Tommie"), gathered together enough old lumber, bricks, and various other pieces of usable material from some of the buildings to construct a unique galley for our use. We built a roof over it to keep off almost all the rain, and we were able to place the galley high enough off the ground to allow cooking regardless of the weather. The finished project amazed everyone: even the Japanese liked to show it when their inspection parties came through. We had space for two callas to prepare the food, and Tommie planted a few bougainvilleas — brought into camp from a work detail — around the outside walls. We were in business.

With the crude facilities in this little shack, we were able to put together whatever was at hand as a special ration of food. At first our menu was limited to the canned milk; later we were allowed to buy, and sometimes the Japanese provided, duck eggs from the Manila markets so eggnogs could be made for the more serious cases that the navy refers to as the heavy sick. As the kitchen prospered into a meaningful activity, we were allowed to buy raw peanuts by the one-hundred-pound sack, with vegetable oil to roast them for an additional source of protein, fat, and vitamins.

An American who had spent her entire active career as a schoolteacher in the Philippines, making her a permanent resident of Manila for most of her life, was untiring in her efforts to supply us with all kinds of extra food. She gathered contributions through many contacts in the city and would literally fight her way past the guards at the front gate to get them in to us. On some days she would be unsuccessful, depending upon the personality of the guard on duty, but undaunted she would be at the gate next day with a calesa full of food, and in her persuasive manner would most generally overcome any opposition.

I am satisfied her unrelenting efforts, over the months she was allowed to operate, contributed to the successful recovery of many prisoners whose lives depended upon additional nourishment. Tucked away in a calesa operated by this woman and a Filipino would be sacks of native sugar, mongo beans, fresh tropical fruits, and whatever bakery goods she could prevail upon her friends to provide. It was all turned over to our diet kitchen and dispensed, as the physicians directed, to those most in need.

After about five or six months of this life-saving mission she was finally refused admission under any circumstances by order of higher Japanese authority. They were suspicious, and with good reason, that she was also a valuable intermediary for current news exchange and written communications with the outside and an active participant in the smuggling of currency into the compound. Her contacts with us were abruptly and perfunctorily terminated.

One of the special features of our diet kitchen was an active culture of yeast we started and maintained. The Japanese agreed to periodically send us quantities of live yeast from the San Maguel Brewery in Manila. With this material we were able to keep our culture going, using rice and native sugar we could then buy. We supplied each man in the wards one-half canteen cup of liquid yeast per day. It provided a most important daily supplement of the B–vitamin complex, which worked miraculously with certain patients.

One had to acquire a taste for the mixture, however; it didn't look or smell appetizing. Not too surprisingly we often encountered patients, obviously suffering from avitaminosis, trading their yeast, or even extra food for that matter, to another prisoner-patient for a cigarette or some native tobacco. We made rigid rules to protect patients from using such poor judgment, but we never did completely overcome this stupid practice on their part.

This lack of prudence was part of a pattern beginning to show up in many prisoners. They seemed to lose interest in keeping themselves clean at a time when soap was still available. If they had shoes, for instance, they would never bother to tie them; they seemed perfectly satisfied to shuffle around in their disheveled untidiness. These patients often had to be physically forced to get on their feet to exercise or get out in the healthful sunlight. They chose to lie all day in their "sack" — rapidly becoming inhabited with countless bedbugs and lice — in a spiritless disregard for personal hygiene. Greediness, selfishness, and miserliness were too often encountered among patients (and other POWs as well) who, as time went on, developed into typical chronic neurotics.

Happily, there were many more cooperative patients who never complained, never gave anyone real trouble, and did not deteriorate into a vegetative state; as soon as the doctor permitted they were on their feet and underway. For the most part they are the ones who survived, but of course it doesn't necessarily follow that those who didn't survive were members of the other category.

Not long after the fall of the Philippines, General Tojo made his triumphal inspection tour of the conquered islands amid all the fanfare that could be milked from the Filipinos. We were aware, as was generally the case with current news, of his arrival through work details made up of patients taken by the guards from Bilibid each day to be employed (as forced labor) by their military in Manila. Seeing the flag-draped streets, the Japanese and Filipino contacts did not hesitate to discuss the nature of the celebration with the POW workers.

The victory parade brought Tojo past Bilibid, where we were amazed, but certainly thrilled, to hear the Filipino band leading the procession strike up the "Stars and Stripes Forever" as they passed the front entrance. The people of the Philippines, noted for their loyalty, in this particular instance, I think, demonstrated courageous daring as well. The occasion gave us all a new sense of appreciation for John Philip Sousa's masterpiece.

One day a large military truck arrived at the front gate with some patients we had been told would be stretcher cases. About thirty GI survivors of the Bataan Death March, who had earlier come through Pasay (from where they had been taken to a work detail building roads in Tayabas), stumbled out of the truck and collapsed, too weak to stand. They were dirty, unkempt, and seriously sick individuals. Many were too ill to help themselves and had to be carried; two had died on the way in, and most of them looked as if the assistance we might be able to give them would be too little and too late.

They related a sordid tale of working with practically no equipment to build a road through a malaria-infested swamp. It was a story of overwork under bayonetted supervision, beatings, and maltreatment of all sorts, including insufficient protection against the weather and disease. Most of the original detail had died. Finally the Japanese, in disgust, brought the remaining ones, who had become too weak to be of any further use, to Bilibid with the reminder that it was our responsibility to get them back into physical condition as soon as possible to assure their return to work.

The prisoners at Tayabas were a working detail, and as such they had received extra food in the form of tinned corned beef confiscated at Corregidor and not considered a particular delicacy by the guards. They had to prepare their rice in what was left of an old wheelbarrow, used at one time in the road-building project. Weakened from malaria and physical exhaustion, they became too weary at the end of the day to expend much energy preparing food in any manner; the cleanliness or physical condition of the utensils they were required to use was beyond any effort on their part to maintain.

In this particular instance extra food was not the sole contributing factor necessary to their survival. We prepared some nourishing soup in the diet kitchen to give them upon arrival, but most were too sick to show any immediate interest in food. I remember trying to serve some soup to one army lad whose home had been in Indiana. We had moved them into the ward, and he was lying in his filthy rags on the cement floor of an already congested area. His only request was for a bedpan to care for his uncontrollable diarrhea and a container in which to vomit. He was one of the most dispirited lads I had so far encountered. He didn't want food; he didn't want anything; in fact, he didn't want to live. With bitter condemnation he told us that his country had let him down and he wanted never to return. He died during the night, so typical of the many hundreds of prisoners during those early dark years of confinement who completely lost all hope in the foreseeable future and, in some cases, all respect for their government, which in their opinion had failed them.

POWs with this outlook died scornfully condemning those at home who had allowed this state of affairs to come to pass in the Philippines. It was a shock to observe our countrymen despairing so soon, losing faith in the future and respect for their heritage. With such a combination of physical debilitation and despondency, we generally failed in our attempts to persuade them to a more optimistic and reassuring viewpoint. It was a disturbing experience, and we felt so helpless in trying to combat it.

Is it any wonder the defeatist expression "Golden Gate in '48" was being quoted so frequently among prisoners? Some of the more cheerful POWs referred to getting back home to the "golden shore in '44." They didn't have in mind the golden shore some would reach during the time of their confinement.

During this period in our sojourn at Bilibid, Yakushiji made his appearance. His English was as good as ours, and he told of being a successful merchant in Seattle who was caught in the Far East when war broke out. He was now acting as a Japanese interpreter and public relations adviser for their headquarters in the Philippines. His mission at Bilibid was to promote a better rapprochement and understanding between the Japanese and the POWs by showing movies once a week with a portable machine. Naturally we were at first encouraged; movies would be a welcome diversion, at least the type coming to mind with his proposal. The films, however, included pictures showing the fall of Singapore, of Hong Kong, and of Corregidor and such other propagandized exposés as their ingenious designs prompted.

Such biased films were insulting to our sense of loyalty, as well as to our intelligence. In one instance a newsreel ended with a clever exposure picturing Japanese soldiers marching over fallen British and American flags. We were of a unified opinion that the photography, for a people whose reputation in this field was considered by many as one of the best, appeared second rate. Many prisoners found courage enough to boo some of the reels. Almost all of us would leave before the finish of the evening's so-called entertainment. The propaganda efforts were not long continued, and Yakushiji's polite attitude of friendliness withered on the vine also.

The Japanese were not the only ones putting out propaganda. Every sick straggler, occasionally brought to Bilibid from a small POW work detail kept at Corregidor, would relate glowing accounts of major successes being broadcast from KGI in San Francisco. These boys had secret access to a radio on Corregidor and of course took full advantage of it. We eagerly absorbed every bit of exhilarating information they would bring in without a serious doubt as to its truth. We thrilled at the president's reported proclamation saying the boys in the Philippines would eat their next Christmas dinner at home; we assumed he had in mind Christmas 1942. We would grasp at any straw that provided a psychological lift.

After a prolonged and frustrating delay, medical personnel were finally paid in printed Japanese pesos, using a scale adapted to comparable positions in their military. We were then allowed to buy limited types of food through a Japanese merchantman in Manila. He would come to Bilibid every ten days or so, solicit orders for whatever was currently available in the markets, and later deliver them to the store we established inside. Generally the produce obtained would be fresh fruit, peanuts, mongo beans, and duck eggs. Inflation soon raised its ugly head; the price of eggs, for instance, finally reached one peso each (a prewar peso represented fifty cents in U.S. currency). After the first year or so, available food from the outside dwindled to such items as tea and other nonessentials, and prices rose to a prohibitive figure.

Being able to buy extra food, even in limited quantities introduced attractive variations in the monotony of our daily routine. Little groups banded together to prepare, according to individual tastes in the group, any produce they were able to buy through the store. Using the cooked issue of rice from the main galley as a base, all sorts of extras with weird titles and descriptions were put together into what was recognized in camp under the Philippine term *quan*. The term was used to identify any combination of foods cooked in the most unusual kinds of utensils and under the most questionable methods of preparation.

Quans (the term also applied to the group of people preparing the food) sprang up all over the place, and the recipes quanned would curdle the stomach and make the hair on the average housewife stand on end. Some innovations were sensible: mongo beans sprouted in dampened cloth or in small window boxes and then served with the rice were among the best. Large tin cans were fabricated into ovens, where all sorts of mixtures were baked with varying degrees of success. The number of quans became limited only by the availability of crudely fabricated electrical appliances for cooking; the Japanese wisely allowed only the two main galley fires to be laid. "What are you going to 'quan up' today?" was a question heard throughout camp each morning.

As the position of the occupation forces deteriorated, our available food in Bilibid eventually reached a semistarvation level. Extra food we bought from the outside market was cut off, leaving us entirely at the mercy of the Japanese quartermaster. During the time we were able to purchase from markets in Manila, Dr. Sartin directed all officers and corpsmen who received the Japanese pesos to volunteer a percentage of their pay into a common fund to buy food for patients and those other prisoners in our camp who weren't receiving any of the printed money. The diet kitchen distributed this extra food.

In November of 1942 we were pleased to receive permission to mail one card to our family, on a printed form provided. They allowed us twenty-five words, but we could not call attention to anything indicating the date, the weather, or our location; in fact we were limited to favorable items of information concerning our POW life and Japanese treatment.

It was difficult to write any but meaningless, stereotyped phrases, and it took some study (we had an abundance of time) to get something worthwhile on the card. Indicating we were alive probably was the most important aspect of the message. The Japanese told us any card, in the opinion of the censors, containing material of a suspicious nature would be thrown out and the writer possibly punished. We knew how painfully suspicious our captors could be, so we carefully avoided wording our messages in a manner to antagonize. I asked Ila to look after the farm at Freeland Corners, knowing such an unusual descriptive location (though factual) could only originate with me, eliminating any misrepresentation.

Another frustrating intrusion we had to endure at Bilibid was "Major Wickedness," an overbearing, obnoxious Japanese army officer who visited us occasionally. He informed Dr. Sartin that America couldn't win the war because our senior officers (obviously including Dr. Sartin) were all worthless old men. He irritated us more than any other Japanese confronting us so far; this fact, along with what sordid pleasure he no doubt received, prompted his unwelcome visit with us in the first place. He was determined to humiliate all POWs and to restrict everything pertaining to our welfare, although he never showed any evidence of authority to follow through. In referring to some very sick patients he observed while inspecting the wards, he scathingly remarked, "They will die, all your men die, very good!"

He was a vitriolic individual with a definite sadistic bent, and we never found out his name, other than his coy reference to himself as Major Wickedness; perhaps his actions could all be attributed to a warped sense of humor. He came too often, although a single visit would have been one too many. His swaggering arrogance was offset somewhat by the glowing Allied reports we then were receiving from KGI through our faithful Filipino friends.

One day the guards informed us some bulk rice had been stolen from their storeroom in the front office building. They made quite an issue of attempting to convince us that stealing, in their opinion, represented one of the worst of crimes. As far as they were concerned stealing was a weakness of all Americans. Later on as POWs, we were to observe that pilfering among themselves or from their quartermaster supplies (or from us) was accepted procedure. It was considered something in the nature of a challenge; if not apprehended, there was no reason for anyone to give the misdemeanor serious thought.

For the present, however, we were all suspect, and the guilty party must be identified so he could be properly punished. If we couldn't or wouldn't apprehend the rice thief, tenko would be called and we would all stand at attention in the hot sun without food until someone did confess. No one came forward to admit his guilt, so we began our vigil standing at kiotsuke in the sun. After an hour or so the poor patient involved did reluctantly confess and was removed by the guard for punishment. Before doing so, he was made to apologize publicly before all of us, according to Japanese discipline. He wasn't punished nearly as cruelly as the poor lad dragged in from Nielson airfield one day and beaten before the assembled POWs with a metal rod. They told us he had lied to the Nipponese.

This display of cruelty was revolting to us when first encountered. It was distressing to see a fellow countryman so brutally punished in a manner we thought would never be tolerated under similar circumstances at home. The POW had no recourse, unless, in trying to resist, he wanted to incite them to a fiendish orgy that their sadistic tendencies often produced. It was a grim situation to witness, but it was much more grim if you happened to be on the receiving end of such a disgusting exhibition.

When the guards would allow them, we did appreciate weekly vaudeville shows produced with POW talent under the supervision of Comdr. Clyde Welsh, MC, USNR. A surprising amount of hidden talent appeared even in small prisoner groups, but circumstances surrounding our confinement were ripe for any inherent talent to blossom. Without equipment, except an old out-of-tune, upright piano the Japanese brought us, we were able to produce some very entertaining shows. All sorts of musical instruments, fabricated by prisoners from scraps of material and imagination, appeared, to the delight of everyone.

Occasionally patients would show up with a violin, or perhaps a clarinet, or, in one case, a trombone lovingly protected during confinement. Of course they were immediately prevailed upon for their showmanship. This required little persuasion, for political maneuvering within a POW camp often was able to keep such a talented patient off the strenuous work detail assignments outside camp. Anything allowing this privilege was sought after by all hands. We were permitted to organize a choir, originally to sing carols for the first Christmas but eventually used in the Sunday church service held under our one mango tree, with Col. Perry Wilcox, army chaplain, in charge.

Almost all of us agreed on the first Christmas Eve, 1942, that it would be our first and last as POWs; we would be singing carols at home on the following Christmas. Dr. Eddie Nelson was inclined to be skeptical, but the pessimists were very much in the minority. Tragically, Eddie would never again have an opportunity to sing carols at home. I organized a quartet of four corpsmen who did excellent work with what music we could write, using the broken-down piano for accompaniment. None of the quartet lived to blend voice in song after the war.

One morning the guards created a flurry of excitement, for after an hour or so of counting and recounting, it was determined someone had escaped during the night. It turned out to be an army patient who managed to get through the wall; there were several places where Filipino notes and food had been exchanged under cover of darkness. The guards wildly indicated all kinds of reprisals would be forthcoming, taking away privileges, etc., but after a few days things quieted, and nothing further developed regarding the incident.

After several months, when the escape was almost forgotten, Dr. Sartin was taken one day to a nearby military prison to interview the recaptured American. We learned he had succeeded in contacting some Spanish friends in Manila who furnished him with the protection of their home and even forged papers allowing him to appear on the street as a Spanish citizen. But he pushed his luck too far, frequenting too many Manila taverns and talking when he should have been listening. Some Filipino, acting as a Japanese informer, exposed him to recapture by the Kempi military police. After months on a starvation diet he was brought to Bilibid to die, as an object lesson to any others who might be planning to escape. He died in a few days, without undue expression of sympathy from his fellow prisoners, a victim of his poor judgment, you might say.

Our daily routine didn't change materially during my stay in Bilibid. We finally accepted and tried to adjust to the drab sameness of its day-by-day existence, reluctantly acknowledging, for the time being at least, that it was not in our power to in any way improve our situation. The rainy season, the typhoons and accompanying floods, the full and waning moons, the tough and not-so-tough guards, the good and the bad days, privileges extended and privileges suddenly taken away, punishments threatened and punishments enacted — all these monotonous events kept us occupied and in so doing helped us to maintain a healthy outlook on the future.

When lights were out and we had no replacement for the few remaining bulbs, we would retire to our beds on the floor and longingly hope for a night of pleasant dreams about home and loved ones. It is not difficult to understand why we looked forward to the period of sleep as the most enjoyable of our twenty-four hours. When it was accompanied by memorable dreams of better days, the hours spent in that fashion were most desirable.

It is difficult, however, to give a realistic description of our immediate reaction upon awakening each morning. There was always that initial shock when the reality of our surroundings flashed through our minds, when we were confronted by four walls and faced with another dismal day as a prisoner of war. Each day we would recall having been deprived of the liberties we had held so dear (but never so dear as now) and look to a future obscured by the personal whims of our sometimes fanatical-minded oriental conquerors. We would remind ourselves how futile it was to entertain any thought that they would react to us as prisoners as we might like them to.

It is not easy to picture convincingly what an effort it was to fight off the sense of despondency that had a periodic tendency to engulf us. Being confined to a small area for a protracted period and surrounded by high insurmountable walls, where even a glimpse of the outside world through the front gate was denied, sooner or later does something to one's personality. Conditions became intolerable in the fall of 1943, and if it hadn't been for the unselfish generosity of Dr. Erickson in sharing a part of his money (smuggled in by friends) to purchase extra food when available, I am convinced my lot would have been much more grim. His steadfast faith and hope for our future boosted the morale of those who came under his influence, rekindling the candle of hope now burning less brightly in many POW hearts.

There were times when confidence would soar to new heights, such as the occasion in the spring of 1943 when we heard through the Filipinos that North Africa had fallen and Italy had capitulated. We now felt it was just a matter of months, perhaps even weeks. Someone recalled the statement of no less an authority than Ludendorf, in his First World War memoirs, predicting the next world conflict being won or lost in North Africa. Germany would now surely fold, or so we thought. Again we grasped at anything upon which to pin our hopes during those days, and we desperately needed reassurance to refresh our courage and determination to persevere.

We had received no information about Allied action in our part of the Pacific; Guadalcanal, yes, but it seemed a long way off, and POW conditions in the Philippines steadily worsened. Serious evidence of deficiency diseases was appearing with increasing frequency in our patients and even among our staff members: eye infections, pellagra, scurvy, and beriberi, in addition to a new painful-feet syndrome now being observed, all symptoms of slow starvation.

Chapter 4

# Eat Rice or Die

Cabanatuan, located some ninety miles north of Manila, became the largest American POW camp in the Far East. It had been a Philippine army training camp before the war and was actually three camps separated by about ten miles. Smith was located in Camp Number 1, nearest to the town of Cabanatuan.

The Japanese had opened it in May 1942. For several months thereafter, disease and death ran rampant, 786 men dying in July alone. Dysentery, malaria, beriberi, pellagra, and vitamin-deficiency ailments weakened the prisoners and were the principal causes of death. Some of the problems had been resolved by the time Smith arrived in October 1943, and the prisoners at Cabanatuan, relatively speaking, were better off than those in most Asian POW camps.

Red Cross packages helped to alleviate some of the vitamin deficiency problems. The standard package contained, among other things, evaporated milk, instant cocoa, sardines, corned beef, powdered orange concentrate, and instant coffee and soup. These packages began to appear on an irregular basis at Christmastime 1942. The containers in which the items came were also valuable, being utilized for drinking, cooking, and a variety of other things limited only by the recipient's imagination.

John Wright, who was incarcerated at Cabanatuan at this time, credited the Filipino underground with helping to improve conditions at the camp by smuggling in goods. He tells the same story Smith does about the guards and punishments. On a happier note, he recalled Christmas 1943, when the glee club toured the camp singing Christmas carols and a midnight mass was conducted.

A few weeks before that Christmas, three postcards reached Sandwich. Besides sending his love, assuring that his health was "excellent" and he was uninjured, Smith requested his wife to save the issues of *Time* and *Life* magazines. The "Red Cross Xmas packages were most welcome," he said, and he told his family not to worry.

Looking for items to put into those packages (chocolate that would not melt in the tropical heat, for example) was one of the more challenging things that the family did during the war years. The task involved some travel and created the fun of filling the packages. Otherwise life on the home front went on as usual in Sandwich, including the highlight of each year, the Sandwich Fair. There had been some talk in 1942 of canceling this venerable event (the fifty-fifth, that year) for the war's duration, but it was decided to continue it.

War-related activities for adults and children included bond and scrap drives, raising victory gardens, practicing blackouts in case of an air raid, observing troop and military trains traveling through town, and Red Cross drives to collect various items. The local newspaper carried a "News from the Boys in Service" column (eventually named more appropriately "News of Men and Women in Uniform"), which kept the home folks informed. There was, of course, some renown in being the family of the town's only Japanese prisoner of war: when news came of Stanley Smith it appeared on the front page of the *Free Press*.

### OUT TO PASTURE AT CABANATUAN

The permanence of a prisoner's billet was anything but certain those days, and our internment at Bilibid came to an end in the fall of 1943. Of his own volition I don't believe a POW would ever volunteer for a new camp — unless his present location was really insufferable, and they were all insufferable to a degree. Of our own choosing we would not have elected to be transferred from Bilibid, but in those days we moved by imperial decree, which controlled our very existence. Dr. Sartin, our commander who had done such a remarkable job under exasperating circumstances, was told to report to the front office. There he was bluntly informed that he and approximately one-half of his present staff would be transferred to another location on the second of October. He would be replaced by a subordinate, Dr. Hayes.

It was not entirely unexpected. The Japanese in charge of prisoner compounds would tolerate only so much in the way of pressure tactics from senior officer members of prisoner groups. Dr. Sartin had relent-lessly pursued all officers with authority who happened into Bilibid. He was always careful to make his demands (perhaps that isn't the term I should use here) relate to the needs of the sick patients. The Japanese staunchly, and with authority, pointed out that the sick re-quired not more but less of everything. After sixteen months of antag-onism they decided, I surmise, the time had arrived to be confronted with a new face and a new approach. Together with some Bilibid patients we were herded into trucks for the ride into northern Luzon, our destination Cabanatuan.

At the railroad station in Manila we transferred to boxcars, about one hundred of us crowded into each one. There was just room to sit or stand but not to move about. Locked inside we continued our 160-kilometer trek over narrow-gauge, rough roadbed, bringing us to a new (to us) POW camp, which in reality was a prisoner work farm. A fifteen-minute stop was made at San Fernando, where, under guard, we surprisingly were allowed to purchase a few food items from Filipinos who crowded around the car doors. One delicacy I recall was pork rind fried crisp. What a welcome change it offered from the rice and weed diet we had been consuming — I was too starved for what it offered to give serious consideration to the probable unsanitary conditions of its handling.

Before leaving Bilibid, we received a soggy rice ball as our day's ration of food, and one who has never tried to eat a cold, sticky, tasteless rice ball cannot begin to appreciate how horrible the en-deavor can be. During a few additional brief stops the train made, some native bananas could also be purchased at five centavos each, and these were greedily seized by the lucky ones nearest the vendor at the car door.

We arrived at Cabanatuan Station in midday and were loaded into trucks for the short journey to the work farm. We were tired, depressed, and apprehensive of our future there. Through the grape-vine we had been told we could expect two things: hard manual labor and working long hours in the fields; however, because of the strenu-ous labor we would get more food than we did at Bilibid. The extra food we sorely needed, but we were not sure the profit side of the ledger would show a net return for the amount of energy expended in acquiring it.

In native Tagalog the description of Cabanatuan would be a barrio in the boondocks. A collection of many one-storied, nipa-palm shacks in a large open field without trees or shrubbery of any sort was our first impression. We were perfunctorily unloaded from the military trucks outside the barbed-wire enclosure and told to spread out all our gear for the usual shakedown inspection. Anything we had been successful in bringing out of Bilibid we now had to maneuver past another searching party. This time POW army officers in charge of the camp (but under control of the Japanese) meticulously probed our personal possessions.

Apparently they felt obliged to function in this capacity, and certainly we preferred not coming under scrutiny of the guards, but there was a question in our minds whether it was necessary for them to pursue the task with such thoroughness. Very bluntly, they behaved in a manner entirely uncalled for in confiscating personal items. Several of us had managed to salvage stainless steel buckets (medical), so convenient as an all-purpose utility article; these we were told had to be turned over to them for general use in camp. Later we saw buckets, suspiciously like ours, being used as personal equipment of the inspection party; they were a big temptation.

Our navy group was finally allowed access to the inner sanctum within the wire enclosure and assigned to one of the various nipa shacks. Fortunately, our officer group was given one with a wooden floor. The barracks' construction was mostly nipa palm, typical of all native housing out here. Almost all of them had dirt floors, although some of the better ones had wooden catwalks down the center, which at least kept the occupant out of the mud during the monsoon season. The bunk where one's gear had to be kept was about a foot off the ground. These elevated bays (or bunks) were built in two levels, one above the other, so if you belonged in the one above, you had to climb a crude ladder to reach it.

Total space allotted to each POW was about three feet by nine feet. The front and rear of the barracks remained open, thus always assuring one of ample fresh air — and, in season, wind as well as rain. Everyone played host to literally millions of bedbugs and lice in the loose bamboo slats and wooden supports. The unsanitary conditions under which we lived made it almost impossible to eliminate them, and their prolific tendencies gave them an advantage, making it most difficult to obtain rest at night. Lice one could quite easily control by laundering often, but they were repulsive things with which to deal.

The bedbugs would hide out in the framework of the buildings, and no matter how often one poured boiling water over his little bay, it would become reinfected from those people around him, who all too often had lost interest in too many things, including personal hygiene.

We were informed soon after arriving that we would be assigned to the daily work details — not to the practice of our profession. Army POW personnel had been designated by the Japanese to operate that part of the camp within the wire enclosure; they could be referred to as *prison command,* if one used the term loosely. We were satisfied in our own minds that the "Inner Circle" had decided before we arrived that there were no openings for any additional navy medical or dental officers on the staff. The ramifications of internal politics in POW camps were fantastic. Staff jobs were the choice details; requiring very little physical labor, they were jealously guarded.

Cabanatuan was the largest prisoner-of-war camp in Luzon, and although it comprised mostly transient POWs, it probably averaged between two thousand and three thousand POWs at all times. Because all inside jobs (meaning inside the barbed wire) did not require work under the guards, as on the farm, these assignments became ruthlessly sought and were more or less given to those who rated with the right (army) people. Our navy group from Bilibid, with the exception of Commanders Sartin, Joses, and Erickson, who were excused because of age, rank, and health, was called each morning to help work in the farm detail. We marched out of the compound to cultivate by hand (literally) the three hundred or more acres the Japanese had designated as a prisoner-of-war work farm.

After a 5:45 A.M. reveille ("revolley," as the English or Australians would say), we would take our mess kit to the galley for our ration of lugao. We had to eat rather hurriedly, for the work details were called at 6:30. Approximately one thousand prisoners went to the various farm plots each day, working with only a pick, shovel, or a large hoe. The clay-like soil was tenacious in resisting any efforts on our part with the equipment provided. We would be assigned in groups of one hundred, each group having a POW camp officer as leader, who in turn was responsible to the guards, who naturally ran the show.

We first assembled inside the barbed-wire enclosure, mustered by our own personnel, then marched out from the inner camp, where the guards would be waiting to take over. We did every type of work coolie labor would be called upon to do, dressed accordingly. We were not allowed to wear anything on our feet, in case any of us had been fortunate enough to have retained a pair of shoes. Our only other apparel was something that served as a shirt and shorts, many times crudely sewed together from all sorts of nondescript material. Ultimately we had to resort to the Japanese G-string. This was our first experience working barefooted; at Bilibid we all wore wooden "go-aheads," a piece of wood with a strap of whatever was available over the top, quite typical of oriental footwear.

Our first day on the farm I was one of a group who marched about a half mile into the field to gather cucumbers. A flat, wood platform, some four feet by eight feet with a handle at each corner, was used as a litter to carry the harvested produce. Four of us were given such a conveyance to be supported by the handle resting on our shoulders. *Camote* (native sweet potato) vines were comparatively light, but cucumbers, when piled as high as the guards insisted, represented a terrific weight upon one's shoulders.

Struggling along with bare feet over sharp cinders and lava rock, wincing with each step while bearing one corner of the litter of cucumbers that first morning, I was as close to physical collapse as I ever want to be. They required us to carry the litter into camp to the guard's office, where scales for weighing in were located; all produce from our labors was sold to the Philippine markets by the Japanese.

Our first load of cucumbers weighed in at five hundred kilos (a kilo is 2.2 pounds). There were times when I thought I would never make it, and the prodding guards probably were the deciding factor in my doing so. If one of us did collapse, many did, and by so doing spilled some vegetables; a healthy kick and a prod by a Japanese bayonet would be the result. With the exception of some badly scarred shoulders and sore feet and muscles, after the first few days we adjusted and carried our share of the load in most cases without too much discomfort. As the weeks rolled on we became toughened to the point where very little grumbling was heard at 6:30 A.M. when the call "All the farm detail" would ring out through the camp, and we would fall into line for another day on the farm.

They allowed us one break of fifteen minutes each midmorning and afternoon. The guards called it *yasumi* (rest period); such Japanese expressions were soon used freely by the prisoners. Aside from the short rest and a noon break of an hour, we worked from 7:00 to 5:00 each day. We didn't work Sunday nor on the days we were blessed with rain. The POW Cabanatuan prayer, one of the many amusing things a prisoner had to originate to keep alive his sense of humor, ran something like this:

> Lord, if it is within Thy power
> Grant us a yasumi shower.
> Then if it isn't too much strain
> Please grant us an all-day rain.

A shower didn't always grant us a yasumi that would allow us to return to camp from the field. I picked *tillelum* stems (tillelum is an okra-like vegetable) many times in the rain. We would be soaked through, and most uncomfortable for hours sometimes, before being permitted to secure for the day and be marched back to our nipa shacks inside the high perimeter barbed-wire fence.

Aside from severe punishment now and then occurring when some guard would become irritated with a prisoner, the work on the farm didn't seriously jeopardize one's health. Quite the contrary. The Japanese would allow only a small percentage of all POWs to be off work each day. Therefore it was a tough job for the U.S. Army medical officer in charge, Dr. Reed, to distinguish at each day's sick call the ones sick enough to be excused from the patient who was goldbricking. There had to be enough POWs available to meet the day's work quota required by the guards, regardless of physical condition of the ones called to work.

Actually, no one in camp was sufficiently strong to be doing the necessary work, and it was generally conceded one had to be just about dead to rate a day off (star quarters). The name "Rigor Mortis" Reed was given to the hardworking dispensary doctor, and there were many who thought they were about to die when he said they were well enough to go back on the work detail.

All camp sanitation was most primitive. Latrines, or "heads" (navy), were the privy, open-air types, barely qualifying as such. Urinals were mostly ditches or ravines, in rainy season generally provided with running water but otherwise simply gullies. One night, after everyone was supposed to have retired, a prisoner, making one of the frequent calls undernourished bodies seemed to require, was accosted angrily by someone at the bottom of the dark, shallow ravine, telling him to be a little more careful!

The disturbance was sufficient to attract a guard making his rounds nearby, causing three army POWs, a major and two captains, to be discovered attempting escape. Using the ravine as a means of reaching the perimeter fence without detection, they encountered a shower of urine, resulting in the angry warning that foiled their well-laid plans, which might have been successful otherwise. As hazardous as the undertaking surely was, the impulsive outburst on the part of the major showed a serious lack of good judgment if the venture were to succeed.

The Japanese in command didn't lose any time making an example of them. They were severely worked over that night, and the following day each one was tied to a post outside the camp entrance located on a main Philippine roadway leading into the province. All Filipinos going by were forced by the attending guard to punish each condemned officer with sticks provided. Whenever the guards weren't too tired, or if they felt the Filipinos were using the cudgel too gently, they would wield as many blows with it as their emotional instability inspired. They would even turn on the poor Filipino if he showed any reluctance to follow their instructions.

This went on for two days without respite, with only sufficient food and water to keep the officers on their feet. The camp was then informed the prisoners would be shot, and "Everyone must see!" POWs were required to dig three graves just outside the wire enclosure in open view of the compound, and on the third morning the victims were brought to the designated area; surprisingly enough they were still able to walk the several hundred yards to the edge of the prepared graves. Each one was given a cigarette, if he so desired, and told he must die. With brutal simplicity the guards raised their rifles, aimed, fired, and all three officers fell back into the prepared graves.

The grave openings were filled by camp workers, and a new ruling for prisoners was immediately established by the Japanese to prevent any such disobedience in the future. The camp was divided into groups of ten, each member co-responsible to the others in his group to prevent escape. In case any member of a group did succeed, so we were told, the remaining nine would be shot. A diabolical arrangement, it had an understandable restraining effect for some time. The frightening aspect of the scheme gave all internees cause to ponder the gruesome potentialities each night as they retired.

With very little supplemental food available from the outside and a ravaging appetite acquired from the work on the farm, I arrived at the point where I could anticipate a mess kit of rice with keen relish, enjoying it to the last kernel. Quite often we were allotted a few camotes as an addition to our rice diet. We harvested hundreds of bushels, but only a small percentage ever found their way to our galleys. This native sweet potato was delicious, providing a tasty variety to our scanty cuisine. Frequently we received camote tips (the first ten inches or so of the camote vine) as a cooked vegetable. It was not considered a delicacy, but we didn't complain, for we ate almost anything under the circumstances. Tillelum was also rationed from time to time and was a most welcome item. We needed the vitamins to be found in all three.

These and many other vegetables were grown in large quantities on the various farm plots. I suspect their sale represented a fair income to the Japanese. Tillelum picking was almost recreation, although we had to bend over in a cramped, uncomfortable position throughout the morning or afternoon as we progressed down each row. However, in that position we could carry on a running conversation with the POW working alongside without being detected. Sometimes, to our annoyance, the guard would appear, unnoticed by the prisoner posted as lookout, and those the guard caught talking would be worked over with a vitamin stick (bamboo club).

We soon learned to know the tough guards, their peculiar whims and weaknesses, and how best to cope with their puerile antics. "Air raid!" was the standard warning when someone noticed a guard approaching. The day's drudgery in the fields passed quickly in conversational chitchat or rehearsing events of happier times with a nearby POW acquaintance. Every topic under the sun was discussed except one involving a pessimistic outlook for the future.

We became accustomed to the primitive pattern of life at Cabanatuan; we especially enjoyed the fresh air and sunshine, the beautiful mountain view in the distance, and the colorful sunsets. Notwithstanding the guan blisters (tropical ulcers so resistant to healing) that developed on our skin, the guards with their clubs and bayonets, the barbed-wire fence enclosure, the diet that only partially sustained us, and altogether too many other POW-borne trials and tribulations, life at Cabanatuan and health in general for most of us was not a subject of serious concern.

Because we lived a most regimented life, with all activity restricted, faced at all times with very rigid scrutiny and supervision, it is indeed difficult to conceive of our having access to daily radio reports of stateside news. This most unusual circumstance is more fully appreciated if one understands the comparative ease with which an alert POW often outmaneuvered the Japanese with whom he was forced to communicate. The outgoing GI carried on a continuous and fascinating palaver, disarming the guards while keeping them entertained. Amazing things were done under the most stringent Japanese surveillance; the POW was quick to utilize whatever advantage he could take of his sometimes naive adversaries.

Thousands of pesos found their way into Cabanatuan almost every week without Japanese disclosure. The bulk of them were for internees who had been living in Manila before being called to active duty in the military. There was a constant stream of written communications of all kinds distributed between prisoners in camps throughout the Philippines. In the face of close personal inspection, they were often carried by patients being transferred, sometimes by clever Filipinos, and not infrequently by an enemy courier. Japanese very often used American prisoners to drive as well as service their military trucks, and this afforded the GI wonderful opportunity to promote extensive undercover traffic between POW camps.

The most astounding, and surely the most dangerous, activity at Cabanatuan was operating the radio ingeniously engineered by POW technicians using bits of radio parts gathered through surreptitious contacts on the outside. In fact many of the necessary pieces were "acquired" from direct contact with the Japanese, who also called upon our personnel to repair their radios. Their equipment seemed to be repeatedly in need of replacement parts — understandable considering the clandestine traffic conducted by the repairman. Only a few POWs knew where our radio was located in camp, and fewer still ever saw it, but everyone was aware of its existence except those who would have torn the place apart had they known.

A roundup of news was released about 9:00 in the evening to a very limited and select group, who didn't lose any time in getting it to the many nipa shacks in other parts of the compound. Hardly anyone turned in at night until he had heard the news, and camp morale rose and fell depending upon the substance of the reports. Some nights those in control of the radio, for various reasons, would consider tuning in much too hazardous, and the newscast was washed out. The guards never uncovered this Cabanatuan radio, although there were periods when its operation had to cease because of suspicion that brought about several unannounced searches.

It was difficult to prevent or disguise a general feeling of excitement and expectancy sweeping the compound when a bit of startling worldwide news of Allied success was circulated from one nipa shack to another. Information concerning almost all major advances by our forces reached us, secluded as we were, about as quickly as their disclosures were made at home. Often fantastic exaggerations would result as the information was retold throughout the camp; sometimes a very insignificant news item would assume unwarranted importance through embellishment by enthusiastic POWs. The morale of the whole encampment seemed to hinge on this little piece of contraband equipment, reportedly built into an army canteen.

Usually it hung innocently enough in plain view of the guards whenever they pulled their surprise inspections. "Beetlebrain," "Donald Duck," "Air Raid," and many other notorious head-cracking guards at Cabanatuan would have had a field day with their clubs if, in their awkward probing, they had ever been able to establish its location or to have been reasonably sure of its existence. I surmise building a radio was so beyond the realm of probability or so far removed from anything they might have undertaken in like circumstances, that the concept remained innocently beyond Japanese grasp of GI ingenuity and daring. Not surprising, either, as much of their hard-to-understand behavior was too bizarre for us to rationalize successfully.

Compassion was not an inherent characteristic of the Japanese military we observed. It wasn't a practice they followed with their own personnel, and they were entirely unsympathetic to our attempts at providing extra food and whatever medication we could for hopelessly sick patients. One day a lock-ward (psychiatric) patient wandered off from under the careless supervision of the corpsman in charge. Every effort was made to find him before having to report the incident. We finally had to acknowledge his absence but called attention to the fact he was a mental case and therefore not responsible for his behavior.

Not unexpectedly, pandemonium broke loose; extra guards were called and, in loud voice, sent scurrying in all directions outside the camp in an effort to apprehend the missing patient. Several hours of exhaustive search in nearby fields failed to uncover him, so the alternative, as they saw it, was to punish the entire camp; presumably we were all responsible. The usual threats were made: no food would be issued until he was brought back, no camp-sponsored entertainments, no more commissary privileges (already *skoshi* [very few]); in fact, there was to be no respite until we had returned this poor, mentally sick prisoner to the clutches of our impatient captors. The corpsman responsible would probably be shot and so would the doctor in charge of the lock-ward, so we were informed.

It was touch and go for the rest of the day; by nightfall, however, things quieted to almost normal — without the returned patient. About five days later he was discovered hiding under a pile of hay being loaded on litters by a farm work detail. As mentally upset as the poor boy was at the time, we never thought he had intended escape, which he somehow had miraculously accomplished. It is more likely that, when the occasion presented, he had simply wandered off and continued to wander aimlessly about the farm at night, existing on whatever raw vegetables he was able to find.

In a frightfully weakened condition he was returned to the camp enclosure with the accompanying noisy excitement of the guards, who immediately ordered a grave to be prepared for his burial: Japanese justice as they interpreted it. Several hours were spent by our doctors trying to convince the sergeant how irresponsible the patient was and how inhumane would be his execution. But their military judgment was not so easily thwarted, so he was pushed into an open grave because he was too weak to stand beside it, and the sergeant in charge emptied his .45 into the fortunately half-unconscious, pathetically helpless body. The doctors had mercifully drugged the patient for the ordeal.

From time to time the guard office would request a list for a draft of prisoners they would transfer to Japan; no one in his right mind wanted to be included. What little clothing we had, sufficient for our needs in the Philippines, was wearing out — not too serious under tropical conditions, but the climate in Japan was anything but tropical. Furthermore, heating prison camps for comfort here was not required; in Nippon the situation would be even worse, and from what we had encountered so far, no one expected the Japanese to put forth any effort or much expense in making us comfortable.

To support our reasoning were stories we had heard from guards about many prisoners dying the first winter in Nippon from exposure and cold. In fact, a propaganda letter had been printed in the Manila paper, purportedly conveying appreciation from an American officer in a prison camp in Manchukuo for the use of a cemetery to bury the POWs who had died there. Rumor had it that five hundred out of an original seven-hundred-man draft to Manchuria died the first winter. Indeed, everyone used all possible means to avoid Japan drafts, and every time a rumor circulated about a list for one being assembled, all available POWs sweated out the possibility that their names would appear.

If a prisoner could walk, he was eligible to go, unless he had a history of dysentery in his record. They seemed to panic at the thought of coming in contact with either tuberculosis or dysentery. Every Japanese, down to the lowest-rated private, was painfully aware of the seriousness of these diseases, which were found extensively in his homeland. Each POW on the list was required to undergo a stool examination before being accepted for transfer to Japan, and it wasn't uncommon practice for prisoners to get a positive stool specimen from an active dysentery patient to use in getting his name removed from a draft.

I like to think Divine Providence moved in our favor in early February 1944, when upon returning to our barbed-wire enclosed quarters from work on the farm one day, we were told of a three-hundred-man all-medical draft being prepared for transfer to Japan. Just why so many medical POWs were requested was never satisfactorily explained; whether it had been required by the Japanese, or whether our own administration considered so many medical personnel in camp a potential threat to the security of their jobs, we could only conjecture. Practically all of the navy medical team from Bilibid appeared on it, together with some of the surplus army POWs.

We were inclined to suspect we were being given "the business," and we were not happy about it. Our own army, however, attempted to reassure us such was not the case. The news the past several days reported Truk in the process of being completely demolished by our naval air force, indicating to those who considered their opinion worthwhile that the Philippines would be next on the list — no doubt within a few months. There was a reasonable chance this would be the last draft of POWs the Japanese would be able to move from the islands, and it was our misfortune to be included with those to be evacuated now. Could we have remained a few more weeks in the Philippines, our rescue would be near, or so we were led to believe.

Analyzed with current information this was the situation, which turned out to be a most inaccurate projection.

Some American Red Cross packages of food had been distributed during the Christmas season; for the past month or so we had enjoyed a taste of home-inspired delicacies with our rice. Small as the portions were, they constituted the most important event affecting our lives since arriving at Cabanatuan. One year earlier we had received a similar box in Bilibid. Unfortunately, there were prisoners who traded their packaged food for the cigarettes, coffee, or tobacco in the Red Cross boxes. Each one needed every ounce of nourishing food he could get, but there remained some whose fuzzy reasoning persuaded them otherwise.

Trading was allowed in camp, except for patients who were acutely ill and considered not responsible. Some of us who didn't use tobacco were much sought after for bargaining. There developed an active commodity traffic. I saw small packages of Kraft cheese sell for thirty pesos, representing $15 at current rate of exchange. Unfortunately, money derived from the sale of nourishing food was often lost in the various poker games so prevalent throughout Cabanatuan. There were other inconsistencies: the uncontrollable appetite of a few emaciated and semistarved patients who determinedly consumed their entire twelve-pound box of Red Cross food in one day, dying before the next of acute indigestion.

We prepared to leave, buying or bartering warm clothing and additional food (or anything else we thought we could use in Japan) from those left behind. We were to depart from Cabanatuan on February 26, stopping off in Manila (hopefully Bilibid) on our way. By undercover dealing I had managed to trade my Hamilton wristwatch to a guard for a sack of mongo beans I am satisfied he pilfered from their military stores. The soldiers were always anxious to purchase American watches or jewelry as the war progressed. Inflation in the Philippines from counterfeit as well as official Japanese currency flooding the markets made the paper money practically worthless, and the guards sought things of material value to send home.

Few, if any, POWs wanted pesos either, but we would readily trade marketable possessions for any food we could get, and of course the Japanese had all the food. Mongo beans were selling in camp, when one could buy them, for five pesos a canteen cup. The sack of beans I received for my watch measured one hundred canteen cups, so the estimated return I realized on my seven-year-old $45 watch was five hundred pesos, or $250 prewar rate of exchange. I traded most of my mongo beans for the more easily transported Red Cross food, starting my journey to Nippon with some extra nourishment stashed away in my duffel bag.

The crucial day that future events would prove to be the most important in our POW lives finally arrived, and although unaware then of what bearing it was to have upon our ultimate survival, we wearily tumbled out of our bunks at 5:00 A.M. from a sleepless night to prepare for the next move. Once again we were going out into a void, leaving behind what little security our brief six months at Cabanatuan had provided. This time we would journey over many hundreds of miles of hostile seas, apprehensive and uncertain about the Japanese homeland of our enemy. Nevertheless, we thought we observed several things indicating this draft was singular.

Their entire attitude toward our departure had been far more conciliatory than on any other occasion. It was noticeable as well to others not on the draft, and many unrealistic but moving stories went the rounds as to why we were being shipped out. One such fantastic tale had us being transferred to Japan to help in the medical care of the civilian population throughout the islands, allowing more of them to be utilized by the military.

One of our army physicians, who had a speaking acquaintance with a Japanese officer at Cabanatuan, approached him to have his name removed from those scheduled to depart. Reportedly, he was informed that were he not to go with this draft, he would regret it as long as he lived. Upon what grounds the officer was basing his opinion is open to debate, but I am sure Dr. Kirschner would verify the statement as being most accurate, evaluated strictly in accordance with events to follow.

We left Cabanatuan without the usual shakedown inspection, and this time our transportation to Manila was by railroad coach. Arriving at Bilibid we found our shipmates, left behind some six months earlier, very depressed and in poor physical condition. We had complained among ourselves how rigorous life at Cabanatuan had been, but in comparison to our fellow inmates here we were in the pink of condition. Our color was better, our weight improved, and our optimism so much more apparent than theirs, even though we were about to embark on a cruise where the odds were heavily against our survival.

Our friends in Bilibid cautiously registered their concern for our safe arrival in Japan. They, too, predicted an early liberation of the Philippines. In their opinion our group would no doubt be the last POWs Japan would try to move through the submarine-infested waters of the China Sea. They hinted it was most unfortunate we had been caught in this predicament at such an inopportune time. Little did they know how fate, within a few months, would destine them to travel the same tortuous sea route we were about to sail, but with a horrendous result. In two successive sailings 75 percent of their number would be decimated by repeated Allied bombings and submarine activity attacking their convoy en route to Japan.

During our stay in Bilibid the Japanese continued the preferential treatment they had shown at Cabanatuan. Extra food was brought to the store to be sold only to our group: bananas, peanuts, and coconuts — food badly needed by Bilibid prisoners also. They hadn't been allowed to purchase food from the outside for months. Fish, eliminated from the diet since we left there, was furnished by the quartermaster on one or two occasions for the general mess.

Work details, escorted daily from Bilibid for menial labor in the port area, brought back information of a large hospital ship tied at the docks on the waterfront, so we began to speculate whether we would be taken aboard for our trip to Japan. There was some reason to think we would because of our professional qualifications, but our better judgment finally convinced us we were becoming naive in this fantasy of preferential treatment. Part of our wishful aspirations stemmed from the sheltered immunity from attack a hospital ship offered. We should have known better after more than two years' experience with our Asian brothers; we were simply carried away with hopeful expectations. The trim, white hospital ship was there all right when we arrived at the pier, but so was an old, ratty-looking tramp merchantman into whose dank hold we were herded as we came aboard.

### SAILING THE HIGH SEAS BELOW DECKS

I can't do justice to the occasion in trying to describe our apprehension as we got underway aboard the Japanese merchantman, severing our ties with the semisecurity of the Philippines for what we desperately hoped and prayed would be a successful arrival in Japan. When we weighed anchor we were apparently sailing without cargo;

the ship appeared to be empty except for the crew, some extra soldiers, our ever-present guards, and a number of Nipponese civilians wandering around the deck.

As we slowly steamed out of Manila Bay our loyalty to the war's effort, I am afraid, didn't include any hope of our submarines appearing to blast this enemy ship out of the water. In fact, I am sure we prayed that Allied air and submarine activity would be reduced to zero until we arrived in Japan. A gnawing feeling of uncertainty gripped us on this eventful morning, overshadowing any optimistic outlook we were sharing with each other down in the ship's black, foul-smelling hold.

We were underway for twenty-three long, bleak, dismal days, setting some kind of record for traveling the shortest distance in the greatest number of days. At any time, day or night, our existence hung in a precarious balance. Twenty-two long nights we listened to the monotonous turning of the ship's engines, nervously listening even more intently when they would be stopped, as they were periodically, for sonar check on Allied submarine activity.

Sleep was out of the question during those tense periods of listening. We reminded ourselves how successful our submarines and aircraft had been in searching this area for just such targets as our Japanese ship presented. Our hearts would beat faster as we realized that at any minute there was the possibility of an explosion ripping open the ship's side. It was always a welcome relief when the monotony of the engines resumed, giving us relative, but only temporary, reassurance.

We were attacked only once. The crew aboard ship, after the excitement subsided, told us a submarine had sunk one of their cruisers covering the twenty-ship convoy, which had scattered at first signs of attack. Fortunately, we experienced rough seas and low-hanging clouds practically the whole trip, and under the protective behavior of the elements it was difficult to work up any sympathy for those aboard who were seasick. It was almost a pleasure feeling a little nauseated, in our circumstances. We zigzagged all over the China Sea in a desperate effort to avoid attack, and I must admit we appreciated the fruits of our captors' successful navigational efforts.

We were allowed one pint of fresh water a day per person. With it we could do as we pleased; that was all we would have for drinking, washing, brushing teeth, or any other need. We were permitted, one at a time, to climb out of the hold onto the deck to use the open-air benjos temporarily rigged for prisoners' use. This was traveling in comparative luxury. POWs coming to Japan after we left the Philippines were forced to use old buckets or any container available in the hold of the ship, where, unemptied, they contaminated the already foul-smelling air under the battened-down hatches. At least we could get on deck occasionally to enjoy a breath of fresh sea air and, when conditions permitted, scan the horizon to observe how many ships might still be in the convoy.

After being underway one week we dropped anchor at Takow, Formosa (now Taiwan). Two days were spent here loading raw sugar in the hold below us, presumably to be converted into transportation fuel, which was then in short supply in the Japanese homeland. We looked longingly at those sacks of sugar coming aboard, for sugar hadn't been available in our diet for months, and we immediately began making plans to pinch as much as we could get hold of for our own use.

The Japanese, in preparing the ship for conveying POWs, had failed to take into consideration a small escape hatch leading from our level to the hold directly ahead of us, providing us access to the loaded sugar. The first night, with several layers of sacks already aboard, we took turns climbing into the ink-black hold, apprehensive every minute about being discovered by a guard who might have been posted expressly for that purpose. We proceeded to fill every sack, sock, mess kit, or any other available container we had with the precious cargo.

To avoid detection, we used what we considered to be an ingenious method. Uncovering a layer of sugar sacks, slitting a small hole in one corner, and draining only as much from each sack as we thought wouldn't be missed, we then replaced the unopened sacks on top. It took a frightening amount of time, handicapped as we were in dense darkness. We were terrified by the thought that each little sound we made echoed and reechoed throughout the entire ship. We had every reason to believe there would be severe punishment if we were apprehended. It was risky, and probably a foolhardy business, but we couldn't resist such an opportunity, and taking it from the Japanese, notwithstanding the hazardous circumstances, was a satisfying challenge.

Stanley W. Smith in Manila just before the outbreak of war in the Pacific. *Courtesy Stanley W. Smith.*

Bilibid Prison. The dotted line in the center is on the wall that separated the prisoners' area from the Japanese quarters. Other numbered areas are as follows: (1) the staff quarters, (2) the diet kitchen, and (5) the guard house. *Courtesy Stanley W. Smith.*

Navy POWs in Bilibid, July 1942. Those identified are as follows: (1) Dr. Cross, (2) Dr. Joses, (3) Lieutenant Kusomoto, (4) Dr. Sartin, (5) Dr. Hayes, (6) Dr. Erickson, (7) Dr. Smith, (8) Dr. Welch, and (9) Dr. Nelson. *Courtesy Stanley W. Smith.*

Cabanatuan POW Camp, November 1944: (1) our "nipa-shack" quarters, (2) Cabanatuan native village, (3) the "farm" plot, and (4) Japanese quarters. *Courtesy Stanley W. Smith.*

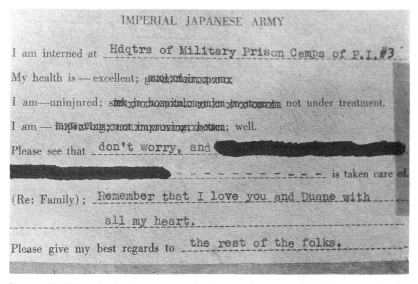

Censored POW card, which was received in Sandwich August 16, 1943. *Courtesy Stanley W. Smith.*

Kobe International Hospital, 1945, in front of No. 2 Ward Block. Stanley Smith (9) is standing in front of his quarters. Others in the photograph are doctors Berley (1) and Glusman (7), who shared his trip to Tokyo, senior officers Page (3) and Akeroyd (8), and Dr. Ohashi (6). *Courtesy Stanley W. Smith.*

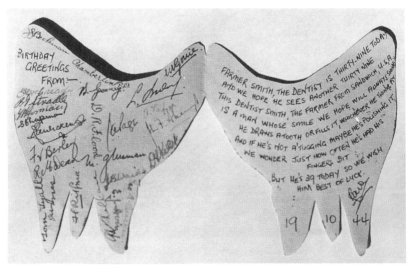

Homemade birthday card, October 19, 1944. *Courtesy Stanley W. Smith.*

Kobe showing the effects of American bombing. *Courtesy National Archives.*

Aboard the USS *Rescue* on the way home. *Courtesy Stanley W. Smith.*

The family reunited. *Courtesy Stanley and Ila Smith.*

# Chapter 5

# Destination Kobe

The Japanese started shipping prisoners to the home islands in 1942, the pace accelerating as the American forces neared the Philippines. The unmarked prison ships too often were floating hells in which the Americans, crammed into the holds, suffered as never before. Unfortunately, too, the ships frequently became victims of bombing or torpedoing by American planes or submarines. It has been estimated that up to five thousand American prisoners were lost at sea or died while the Japanese tried to move them.

Smith, as he mentioned, was lucky the weather was bad; it deterred attack, and his trip turned out to be one of the better ones. Arriving in the port city of Osaka on March 26, 1944, he and another naval dentist, Wade Morgan, began providing emergency dental treatment for the needy prisoners of war in this latest camp, which had had no access to dental treatment for more than a year. The few instruments Smith and Morgan possessed had been smuggled in from the Philippines.

Two months later he was ordered to Ichioka Stadium Hospital in Osaka, which he graphically described as "absolutely the most unsanitary, filthy, miserable, death-dealing hole that I witnessed as a Japanese prisoner." Then, in less than a month, on July 20, Smith was moved in order to help organize and put into operation a "so-called international POW hospital in Kobe." Conditions there were somewhat improved, and patients were brought in from all the other "work camps" in the Kobe-Osaka area.

Osaka and Kobe were major industrial and port centers located on Osaka Bay. Osaka's population of 3,394,000 was second only to Tokyo's; sixteen miles west, the smaller Kobe (with a population of more than one million) had a decidedly cosmopolitan and international atmosphere because of the many foreigners who had settled there beginning in the nineteenth century. The situation here was not good for either the prisoners or the Japanese civilians because in the closing months of 1944, American submarines were dealing crippling blows to the Japanese merchant marine, thereby creating shortages of almost everything. To make matters worse, the winter of 1944 to 1945 was the coldest in more than half a century.

In Sandwich, Smith's wife received news of her husband from an unexpected source in April 1944. An American naval officer, M. H. McCoy, who had escaped from Bilibid back in October 1942, wrote, "I recall your husband quite well and he was quite alright the last time I saw him." The first news from Japan came from an unofficial short-wave broadcast the next September: "I am well. Now pleasantly working in a new well equipped beautiful hospital for prisoners of war here. Love and devotion I send you . . . " Further news came in November from an American Red Cross interview with a delegate of the International Committee of the Red Cross: "Lt. Smith, without complaints, can truthfully say camp command exerted itself in creating very satisfactory, efficient hospital, nicest, best equipped most beautifully located hospital he saw since capture."

The last message during this period of captivity came in December. The telegram read:

> [The] following enemy propaganda broadcast from Japan has been intercepted:
>
> I have received reasonable and kind treatment from the Nipponese Army both in the Philippines and here in Japan. My health fortunately has been and is good. . . . Daily I look forward to that happy reunion at home. . . . The hospital barracks is located in a beautiful scenic space at the foot of some mountains. The Nipponese Doctor in charge is kind and considerate of the patients and the staff welfare at all times. I have equipment and supplies and no restrictions are made for all emergency dental treatment of patients here and I'm kept busy. Christmas greetings and love to you all.

### ASHORE AT MOJI

The sugar episode had its amusing angles, too — one corpsman replaced half the contents of his navy sea bag with it, hoping to have plenty when he was settled in whatever prison camp we would be located at. Everyone, of course, filled all available small containers.

I, for instance, had several one-pound, empty Klim cans from Red Cross food bargained for in the Philippines. These I filled along with a navy bandage container. Every POW on the ship ate all the sugar his constitution would tolerate the rest of the way to Japan. Still, we arrived at Moji with an abundance of the sweet stuff in our possession; Crawford had better than a third of his sea bag remaining.

Near panic spread through our group when we lined up on the dock, upon getting ashore, and were told to spread out all baggage for inspection. We had relied upon our immediate departure from the "sugar ship" and covering perhaps several hundred miles inland to a POW camp before encountering a shakedown. It was a poor gamble, but with sugar as the stake we could risk taking the chance. I began to have second thoughts about the price we were ultimately going to pay for our sugar as we prepared for inspection. We had undergone so many, some cursory, others in minute detail, and we had learned to start out by exposing only those things we had reason to believe would be acceptable, covering everything else with clothing or other innocent items.

We were greatly relieved, standing alongside our motley array of personal odds and ends, to observe this inspection being conducted by customs officials. The blue-coated little inspectors wanted only to stamp all games, and particularly playing cards, we brought into Japan. We were so thankful upon easing out of what we thought was developing into an embarrassing confrontation. It amazed us, however, under rigid restrictions imposed by war, to find military prisoners searched only for playing cards for official stamping, a routine customs procedure.

Strange it may have appeared to us, but I do know our blood pressure quickly returned to normal. Our sugar, and the knowledge of the unorthodox method by which we obtained it, was safe, for the time being at least. We shouldered our duffel bags and were marched several blocks through Moji to an unheated armory, where we waited all day in the unaccustomed cold for a train at 9:00 in the evening that would eventually bring us to our assigned destination.

The next unpleasantness after our customs inspection at Moji was the appearance of a Japanese army medical officer to inform us he was in charge of our group; in fact, he beamed, he was in command of all prisoners in the Osaka-Kobe area. "I, Doctor Nosu, speak English poorly, understand very well. I opulate [operate], and I teach you doctors; you no good I send you to the mountains. I speak Deutschland, go to Deutschland medical school; English, American schools no good! Deutschland medical schools, number one. I teach you!" He was a fearfully wild-looking individual. He didn't converse in a normal manner: he worked himself into a shouting frenzy, acting for all the world like a maniac.

How to handle an emotionally unstable officer in command remained the primary issue, for it would appear, if we could believe what he said, that we were stuck with this eccentric character for some time to come. He was temporarily subdued, and I suspect somewhat surprised, when two of the physicians in our group, Murray Glusman and Paul Roland, started a conversation with him in German. They discovered the only "Deutschland" he knew was limited to a few stock phrases anyone could acquire with little effort — outside Germany. He very quickly dropped Deutschland as a topic of conversation.

A reliable Japanese source disclosed to us later that he received his medical training at a third-rate medical school in Nippon and was considered even less than a third-rate doctor by his own colleagues. As for his qualifications to "opulate," his alleged ability was as phony as the term he used. After we had become established, Dr. Roland, a qualified army surgeon, took Nosu in hand in an effort to teach him some elementary principles of surgery. He nevertheless, fittingly enough, was given a diagnosis of insanity and committed to a Japanese asylum at the Allied War Crimes Trials after VJ Day.

Suffering from the cold, half-starved, discouraged with Nosu and his tactics, and wearily weighted down with our gear, we stumbled along from the armory that night marching several miles to the railroad station. Nosu, in his warm military overcoat, was harrying us at the head of the line, with guards prodding us on in the rear. But like all struggles we had so far successfully withstood, thinking we wouldn't, we made it to the station. Amid untold confusion, including contradictory orders from Nosu, we boarded a train, our destination a work camp in Osaka, so we were told.

Knowing we were in Moji, and having been told it was connected with the Honshu mainland by underwater tunnel, we anticipated our route to be a novel experience. However, we hadn't taken into consideration the unusual antics of our friend Nosu. He required us to lower all the shades in the coaches because of the blackout, so he said. We were not allowed lights inside the coaches either, making the trip through the tunnel a complete washout — and as complete a blackout as was ever accomplished in Japan, I dare say.

Somewhere in Japan during the night we had to change trains and were hustled to another station, much larger, where we stood for an hour waiting in the cold. The funny little trains in use during the war were pulled by coal-burning steam engines, appearing almost like miniature trains to us. While we waited on the platform, one arrived and proceeded to unload *takusan* (many, many) strange-appearing little white boxes, containing returned ashes of war dead, we surmised.

Nosu became violently excited when he discovered we were watching the formal handling of the boxes (we should have known better). He screamed several orders in Nipponese to Dr. Jack George, who quite naturally interpreted them as meaning we should come to attention to show respect, and he so ordered us. Nosu looked as if he was about to have a stroke; he wanted us to turn away from them — it was insulting to have us gaze in their direction and appear interested. We were shoved around in a rough manner by the guards, and Jack was worked over a bit by the frenzied Nosu, until we finally got organized away from the scene with the little white boxes.

### IN COLD STORAGE AT TSUMORI

The next day at noontime, after a several-hundred-mile ride into the Japanese countryside, we arrived at Osaka. We were loaded into army trucks after being read an imperial rescript ordering us to a work camp in the Osaka area called Tsumori. It was located in the heart of the huge shipbuilding and industrial part of Osaka. The trucks brought us to the front of a large group of unpainted buildings erected in the midst of about twenty tall cement smokestacks. We later learned they represented one of Osaka's main industries. Our first reaction was to assess our chances in a bombing raid, which we were convinced wasn't to be long in arriving.

They escorted us inside bleak and dismal Tsumori to some drab-looking wooden buildings built on the soot-covered, cinder-strewn ground. A young-looking Eurasian, dressed in a fatigue outfit very similar to some worn by better-dressed POWs, stepped up while we were waiting inside, saying in perfect English: "Put your gear over here, fellows, and the commanding officer will be here in a jiffy to speak to you."

From his looks, actions, and speech, possibly because we were tired from our Nosu-indoctrinated trip, all of us mistook him for one of the POWs who were confined here. Jack George approached him in a friendly manner, put out his hand saying he was Dr. George, U.S. Navy, and we were glad to make his acquaintance. His hand was left dangling, and he was curtly informed he was talking to Mr. Fujimoto, the Japanese military interpreter for Tsumori, and he couldn't fraternize with prisoners. So with red faces and frustrating embarrassment, we made contact with our first American-educated Japanese in Nippon working for the emperor.

Fujimoto knew all the answers, making it extremely difficult to pull any POW shenanigans. Fuji was in the habit of telling us he was going to establish a business in South America after the war; the U.S., in his opinion, had lost its attractiveness. He never admitted being in the United States except to visit; supposedly his flawless English was acquired from schooling in Nippon. He was a slick one all right, not worthy of trust by us, nor his own patriots, we were to find out later. His Nipponese was so inadequate he couldn't take dictation rapidly enough to keep up with Lieutenant Nabi, his commanding officer. He would begin to transcribe in Japanese, but invariably change to English as he progressed.

It was obvious his coworkers in the front office were not particularly friendly toward him, for Fuji kept his personal shaving gear, and other items, in one of our barracks. He had shifty eyes that would never focus on you in conversation. He was as native to San Francisco or perhaps Seattle as the latest colloquialism there could make him, and his family background, in our opinion, was not wholly Japanese. He had spent more years in the States, we were convinced, than he had in Nippon.

At Tsumori they really poured it on: military drill every day in Nipponese, intermingled with general roughing-up and occasional face-slapping incidents for those who were slow to comprehend. We were repeatedly informed it would be in our interest to volunteer for work in the shipyards nearby. Although other POWs in camp were required to do so, the officers and medical corpsmen so far had successfully resisted. We countered with a proposal that we were available anytime for professional duties, but according to the Geneva Conference, medical personnel could only be assigned work involving the care of the sick.

They responded by giving us additional military drill and such demeaning jobs about camp as cleaning out the benjos, the contents of which they used as fertilizer. One feature of the harassment program was to provide us with worn-out native brooms each morning, and, escorted by guards, we would be forced to sweep the street outside the camp in view of passing civilians — all a part of a plan to bring us to terms.

Wade Morgan, the other navy dental officer in Tsumori, and I convinced the authorities we could serve a more useful purpose caring for the teeth of POWs so badly in need of attention. Agreeing, they supplied limited material, including zinc oxide and eugenol and some tablets to make our own local anesthetic. Once a week they would lend us two forceps and an elevator for extractions. Inadequate as we felt the equipment to be, the guards soon called on us to provide dental treatment for some of them. A delicate situation, but it wasn't diplomatic to refuse. *Itai, itai* (painful) was the trend of their limited conversation with us.

At Tsumori we were billeted with British, Dutch, and Australian POWs for the first time. They came to Japan as prisoners from Hong Kong, Malaysia, and the Dutch East Indies. Here for the first time we could compare how other POW nationals fared. I suppose it was inevitable, mingling so closely, that personalities would clash — particularly British and American, although the British at Tsumori were greatly in the minority. I can now appreciate why the Dutch have been proclaimed the world's best colonizers; they relinquish so little and expect so much. I can also appreciate the origin of the quip, "That beats the Dutch!" One has to be resourceful indeed to get ahead of the strong-willed sons of the Netherlands.

But I found many good friends among all of them (including the Dutch), and no doubt their opinion of Americans in general was even less complimentary, for they had good reason to complain. We had some sorry examples of native sons represented at Tsumori. After two and a half years traveling the POW road I suspect it would have been naive to expect otherwise.

Amusing enough in retrospect, after carefully rationing our precious contraband sugar all the way from Formosa across Japan, we were terribly upset and disgusted to have it taken from us in the shakedown inspection at Tsumori; the windfall was relished by Lieutenant Nabi, Fujimoto, and the guards, I am sure.

We suffered considerably from the cold damp climate of Japan the first few months after our arrival. Several years in a tropical climate made this weather feel more severe than it would have under more normal conditions. Heat for the buildings in Japan is provided according to a date on the calendar, which may or may not have any bearing on local weather conditions. We arrived in the spring, a time of year when the calendar dictated heating the barracks was unnecessary. Any prisoners remaining in camp throughout the day spent a miserable time in the cold, heatless shacks, moving about as much as possible to keep comfortable. Their answer to our request for extra warmth of some type was short and to the point: we could go to work at the shipyards to keep warm. However, when the workers returned from the yards, charcoal for the little hibachi heaters was generally provided in limited amounts during the early evening hours.

Nosu had established a rule requiring all prisoners and any patients able to stand to open all windows and doors upon arising in the morning, then, baring their chests, to go through vigorous massage (including their backs) with dry towels to "make them strong and prevent pneumonia." A slow starvation rice diet that had brought about a poor resistance in all POWs, together with living in barracks where the temperature range was 30ºF to 45ºF almost all the time, made the plan a lot of nonsense. In their present physical condition most patients had little enough energy to lift a towel; wielding it vigorously was simply unworthy of serious consideration.

I put on all the clothing I possessed, continually moving about the unheated barracks and outside (when there was sunshine) trying to ward off the paralyzing effects of the raw, moist air penetrating everything. Influenced by the extreme conditions of our environment I made a resolution that were I to survive the hardships we now were experiencing here, I never again would want to live where I had to struggle to keep warm. Had we been in good physical condition and provided with a reasonably sufficient diet, we could have easily withstood the weather. We looked forward to warmer spring days and to being liberated before having to spend another cold season in Japan, where we thought our present hardships would be too much to endure.

We welcomed the evening hour when we could crawl into our sacks. Each day we painstakingly assembled them in a manner to get the maximum warmth on the tatami mat covering the floor of the barracks. As the night wore on and we would become warm enough to sleep a few hours, the next shift of loudly jabbering guards would appear, continuing their harassing tactics by noisily shuffling through the building with flashlights to assure that no one had escaped. Where any escaping POW could possibly go in this vast, ocean-encompassed expanse of heatless (and at the time almost starving), hostile country was beyond the comprehension of any poor, sick prisoner. The guards thought otherwise, one could rationalize from the annoying schedule of around-the-clock surveillance.

Many times in the middle of the night we would be routed out and told to stand at attention so we could be counted, assuring Lieutenant Nabi of our continued presence. It was exasperating, but not nearly so much as the oppressive cold we had to endure constantly. We had adjusted to rice in the tropics, but here much lower temperatures, without extra nourishment to produce additional energy, required further adjustment, and some constitutions had reached the limit of further compromise. With increasing regularity we carried the remains of these poor souls to a little crematory near Tsumori, from which the camp later received a small box containing their ashes.

Tsumori was a painful introduction to Japan but only a prelude to more horrible experiences looming over the horizon for some of us in our next move. We had been hearing vague rumors of a new POW hospital being organized at Kobe. In fact, Colonel Murata had given us a propaganda speech to tell us about it, claiming among other things that the Japanese authorities were spending thousands of yen each year to buy bones for our soup (so far none had shown up in our mess). We who would be selected for this hospital were indeed fortunate, so he boasted. Soon it would be ready, and there we could take a bath once a week; his poor family, he lamented, could only have a hot bath twice a month, for "there isn't now sufficient wood to heat the water."

This was quite an admission from the colonel; almost any Japanese would go without some food rather than limit his hot baths. In this land of hibachi-heated homes probably the only time they are comfortably warm is while ensconced in a hot bath. It must be said in their behalf, however, that they are a scrupulously clean people. Reliable stories tell of older Japanese men living in the mountainous areas who spend almost all of every day during the winter months lounging in their hot baths fed by naturally heated springs; others tell of Nipponese children given five and six hot baths a day to offset the cold.

The Japanese have a fond attachment to these baths, and after living there I can understand why. The warmth from a kind sun and from the warm springs in the mountains is looked upon by the masses as something associated with divine blessing, hence their worship and prayers offered to the sun each morning. I, too, greeted the sun with thanksgiving each day and relaxed in its warmth at every opportunity, but my thanks for its delightful radiance was offered to a different source.

### TEMPORARILY DETAINED AT ICHIOKA

After four months of propaganda buildup, three navy medical officers, myself as the dental officer, and six corpsmen were selected to leave Tsumori, being informed we would help staff this wonderful (their term for it) new International POW Hospital at Kobe. There was to be a delay in the ultimate completion of their plan, so we would temporarily be detained at Ichioka, another camp en route.

Arriving at Ichioka, located in Osaka, represents a milestone in my POW experience. Here we reached an all-time low, after which, no matter what conditions we should encounter ahead, they almost certainly had to be better. Food, maltreatment, congestion, corruptness of guards, vermin, and general wretchedness reached a level I doubt was duplicated in any other POW confinement in Japan. How temporary it would be was our chief concern.

To create this infamous domicile of torture for POWs, the Japanese army had boarded the sides under a stadium as a place of confinement. The heat was suffocating in the summer, even as the dampness and chill of the winter months had been merciless. When we arrived in June, the threat of air raids, located as we were in the heart of the Osaka industrial area, was becoming more of a reality. Consequently what few windows were available for fresh air were covered each night at sundown with black air-raid curtains of heavy material. Lack of air movement during the night, together with accumulated heat given off from the cement above, made it almost insufferable; sleep, with countless mosquitoes swarming over one, was next to impossible.

Hundreds of British, Dutch, and Americans had died here during the past two winters since this stadium hole had been conceived. The Japanese, probably from a public relations viewpoint, had never bothered registering it with the International Red Cross. They had used it, according to British POW opinion, to transfer prisoners whom they thought it might be more convenient to have out of the way — permanently, if possible. Classic examples were the British survivors from the ill-fated *Lisbon Maru,* who had been allowed to flounder in the icy waters off Shanghai for several hours before finally being picked up by other vessels in the convoy. After spending precious survival time firing at the prisoners as they struggled in the water while the ship on which they were being transported to Japan was in the process of sinking, the Japanese finally turned their attention to recovering the few still remaining afloat.

At Ichioka the wildest sort of treatment had been prescribed for sick patients. *Moxa,* an age-old panacea prepared from the leaves of certain Chinese plants, was used on POWs in an attempt to eradicate the various diseases resulting from malnutrition. A Japanese doctor would designate primary locations on the anatomy of the poor ailing victim, where little cones of the dried material were to be placed, lighted, and allowed to burn themselves out. It was administered as a treatment for beriberi, pellagra, and painful feet, so prevalent among POWs.

Although brutally uncomfortable, the patients submitting to this ridiculousness would survive, but for the rest of their lives, as a reminder of the practice, they would carry moxa scars on their bodies as a result of the questionable procedure. When moxa failed, the surgeons took over to perform a sympathectomy, requiring much more skill than they were generally able to demonstrate. Horribly mutilated abdomens and incontinence frequently resulted from this experimentation, but the prevailing manifestations of beriberi remained unchanged.

The complete picture of suffering would have to include some description of the painful-feet syndrome; the British preferred the term *electric feet.* By whatever title, it represented one of the most frustrating and difficult ailments to treat successfully of almost all deficiency diseases. For one thing, the clinical picture was without diagnostic symptoms during its early stages, and because of this many sick individuals were forced to continue working when not physically able.

Our doctors had very little clinical experience from which to draw; apparently, the deficiency disease attacked the nerves and blood vessels of the extremities. It produced constant and excruciating pains that were somewhat relieved by exposure to cold water or cold air. As long as the sufferer remained in the tropics — and this held true for the cases diagnosed in the Philippines — exposure to the cold elements did not seriously endanger the patient; tap water was probably the coldest element at hand.

At Ichioka the winters compounded the problem. Because the feet and legs were most generally involved, it was natural to find the patient confined there walking around all day with bare feet on the cold cement and in the frosty out-of-doors, seeking relief from his painful discomfort. Gangrene eventually developed, resulting in the loss of toes and sometimes feet. In a few extreme cases the gangrene eroded tissue and bone sufficiently far up the leg to necessitate complete amputation. The pain, as the disease progressed, was so aggravating that even the disastrous result of exposure to frostbite did not always deter the afflicted from seeking the only immediate relief at hand.

Physical abuse was the rule, not the exception, at Ichioka, and Cato, one of the guards, was exceptionally well qualified to follow the rule to the letter. Before the war Cato no doubt was a bootblack, or possibly a night-soil collector — if such job classifications existed in Japan. At any rate his intelligence wasn't good enough to warrant his being assigned to combat duty, but it was quite sufficient for qualifying as a guard for POWs at home. Cato was without question a sadist, and probably for the first time in his life he had victims who could offer no resistance.

Cato-san was smaller than the average Japanese, probably accounting for an inferiority complex motivating his evil intentions. How much satisfaction he derived from his behavior one can only surmise, but his escapades among POWs were an experience those of us who came in contact with him will long remember. From all appearances Cato thoroughly relished his work, and with equal passion he obviously held all prisoners under his observation in contempt. He epitomized the most offensive of all Nipponese privates ever to have close supervision over us; the arrogance with which he executed his duties was paralleled only by his stupidity and evident lack of compassion.

To appreciate Cato at the height of his career with us, one must picture him during one of his sadistic sessions. Our living space in the Ichioka stadium, including the few feet allowed for limited exercise behind a wall, was so small it was almost impossible to get away from Cato and his henchmen guards during the entire day. It seemed that every time we turned around a guard confronted us, and more often than not it was Cato or Bando; both seemed to be vying for some sort of sadistic honors.

This particular night Cato had the duty, and circumstances during the day had more or less precluded a lively scene at evening tenko. Approximately every two weeks we would be issued a ration of fish, generally too rancid and stale to be palatable; the only other fish included the usual small, slimy ones having to be cooked whole. The fish on this eventful day were unique: fresh and large enough so each prisoner would have a reasonable serving. The guards were attracted to them also (quite a common occurrence) and decided to carry some home to their families. Cato proceeded to pick about twenty of the choicest to be divided among them, which meant POW servings would be reduced severely. Every day they pinched about twenty percent of the grain ration to take home also; all families in Japan had begun to feel the serious shortage of food.

Dr. Akeroyd, Australian Army, our Ichioka senior officer, was encouraged to complain, diplomatically of course, to the Japanese military in charge of the guards. Some of us were convinced that resistance applied at the right time, and in the right manner, might work. Dr. Akeroyd, who had suffered under them all the way from Rabaul, knew better; in fact, he had had the knowledge pounded into him very convincingly several times. But for the benefit of the new arrivals he would try again and so presented himself before Sergeant Okano in the front office.

Akeroyd explained how each prisoner at Ichioka was sick and desperately needed every bit of food, particularly protein, that could be obtained. Today, he continued, twenty fish had been taken from us by the guards, so the sick patients would have less to eat than the Japanese in command had intended. Okano, in his oiliest manner, said he was unaware of any irregularity, would investigate the matter, and take steps to correct it. At the time we had every reason to believe two of the best fish were wrapped in a newspaper, ready for him to take home to his family in the little black cloth bag almost all Nipponese carried. But he smilingly promised Akeroyd to take care of the situation — and he did!

Each night an air of uneasy expectancy surrounded evening tenko, but tonight everyone seemed to sense from the action of the guards that something special was being cooked up for the POWs. Without exception, tenko was always a time of tension for all prisoners. Twice daily we had to assemble, bow, count off, and give a report in Nipponese to a smirking guard, who generally stood before us with bare feet protruding from his worn-out house slippers. We were informed on many occasions that this was a very formal military presentation to him and the emperor. However, it afforded any guard who happened to feel in the mood an opportunity for hazing prisoners.

On this particular night, tenko arrived with more than the usual apprehension expressed on the face of each POW. Everyone was careful to check his personal appearance. The rule established by the Japanese stated all buttons on one's attire must be fastened (it didn't matter how dirty or bug-infested you might be); all buttons had to be buttoned as a signal of respect to authority. So everyone was on the alert when tenko sounded, snapping to a stiffer than usual *kiotsuke* when Cato arrived to receive Dr. Akeroyd's report. When Akeroyd finished, ending with the customary low bow, the fireworks started.

While in this oriental position of respect, the good doctor received a stinging blow on the side of the face from a belt Cato had been holding behind his back. As if it were a prearranged signal, the other guards entered with their belts, and Cato, with a fiendish bellow, proceeded to maul Akeroyd about the face. Cato gave his attention to the officers, with special treatment to the doctor who had interceded for the prisoners; the other guards wreaked their vengeance on the enlisted men. This exhibition went on, varying in intensity, for about two hours, with everybody standing at attention. In between spells the guards would parade up and down before the line of POWs ranting in Nipponese. No one needed to ask why this punishment was being meted out, and no explanation was ever forthcoming.

There was hardly a soul in the place the next day whose eyes weren't swollen and whose face, arms, and shoulders didn't show the results of the night's inquisition. No one at Ichioka ever again raised the question about guards snitching prisoner-of-war rations. When the contents of some Red Cross boxes arriving from the States were strewn on the floor for the guards to take what they wanted first before turning the remnants over to POWs, resentment on the part of the men in camp was well shielded from our "benefactors."

Fortunately, our confinement in this vermin-infested place was relatively short. Shortly before we left, Dr. Ohashi took over as the army medical officer in charge at Ichioka and from the start seemed to show a real interest in bettering the conditions under which the patients existed. He informed us that Ichioka was being abandoned, and within weeks we would be moved to a former American mission school in the residential section of Kobe — the new International POW Hospital finally emerging. Doctors and corpsmen who were to staff this Kobe hospital were being assembled from various British, Dutch, Australian, and American prisoner-of-war camps in Japan. We were hopeful about this newest move, for Dr. Ohashi convinced us he was sincere, although any place other than Ichioka would have to be an improvement.

At Ichioka our seriously ill tubercular patients were placed on the floor in filth alongside others not so sick, who in turn were sleeping alongside and breathing the same air as all other POWs. We were crowded together in a most unhygienic environment, and we hoped for some improvement at Kobe, at least some fresh air, sunshine, and sufficient space to segregate our contagious cases. Dr. Ohashi assured us of these important changes, and I suspect by July 1944, those who controlled the destiny of Japan could see the inevitability of ultimate defeat and thought perhaps it was time to begin putting their POW house in order.

### KOBE INTERNATIONAL POW HOSPITAL

Our arrival at Kobe Hospital was the first occasion since our initial internment by the Japanese that the oft-repeated promises of improved conditions bore some evidence of becoming a reality. Our food improved, for one thing; *daikons*, actually large white radishes so popular and available as a vegetable in Japan, appeared quite often in our diet. One must live on nothing but unseasoned rice for about three years to appreciate how tasty radishes can be when made into a soup. Mixed with the rice, they provided a welcome change. On some days when daikons were not available, a small issue of miso, a very salty, fermented paste made from crushed soya beans, would be issued as an addition to our meal (*miso-shiru*). It was surprisingly good, and our only complaint was not getting enough.

Before leaving the subject of ingredients provided as food flavoring, I should mention that we occasionally were issued, and were frequently allowed to buy, fish powder from the waste products of the vast fish-canning industry. The rancid, nearly spoiled fish we usually received were delectable morsels compared with this odorous fish product. It didn't taste like anything we had ever been issued as food and wasn't in the same class with the black, pickled seaweed that is a culinary achievement in the Orient. The seaweed we did enjoy whenever it was made available to us; it is a healthful supplement in anyone's diet.

Literally every grain of rice, or rice and Korean millet, made available to us was consumed with relish, prepared by our cooks in the usual manner. If a grain happened to fall onto the floor it was immediately retrieved and eaten, its life-sustaining properties so important. The Dutch, in order to prolong the period of eating, having convinced themselves they would thus derive more nourishment from their food, would separate their partly filled bowl into small rice balls about the size of a large marble. Over a period of hours they slowly ate one ball of rice at a time. It tells you something about the Dutch, for only they had the willpower and determination to put such a tantalizing plan into operation and convince themselves it actually had merit from a nutritional standpoint.

Each convalescent patient, and staff member as well, became so desperately hungry that individual measuring of the cooked food issued by our people at mealtime was so jealously watched as to become an obsession. One camp in Japan viewed it seriously enough to rig an awkward but somewhat reliable balancing device so the infrequently available soya beans or fish issue could be apportioned to each staff member and patient equitably. It is difficult to imagine one soya bean becoming so important in the life of the individual, but it also is most difficult to imagine being a prisoner of war for three years with nothing appetizing to eat but rice, rice, rice, three times a day, generally without seasoning.

We were allowed more living space at Kobe Hospital. It included three separate, wooden-frame buildings located in a yard containing some grass, flowers, and trees. The drab, barren factory areas of previous locations had all but convinced us the much-heralded natural beauty of Japan was a fantasy. We enjoyed the attractive view our position above the city afforded us, looking out over the surrounding high board fence to the bay below and the mountains behind us. Our buildings had only an occasional hibachi for heating, and we still had to sleep on the floor, but it was such a welcome improvement over what we had experienced in Nippon that no one seriously complained. Some medical and dental operating equipment awaited us at Kobe, and obsolete as most of it turned out to be, we appreciated receiving it.

It is my considered judgment, based upon observation and care provided POW patients for a period covering more than three years, that our low-calorie, nonprotein, vitamin-deficient and nearly sugar-free diet had no deleterious effect on the teeth and their supporting structures. Certainly we saw less incidence of decay during this period than would have been expected under more normal conditions, and I firmly believe the total elimination of refined sugar in our diet was the controlling factor. A few cases of Vincent's infection and scurvy were diagnosed during the early days, but then both seemed to be arrested for the duration. Most of our trouble involved old, chronically infected teeth flaring to acute levels (possibly as the result of lowered resistance in undernourished bodies) or the fracturing of old, irreplaceable fillings.

Apparently Kobe was the only POW hospital of its type created in Japan. Lacking almost everything normally required in an approved hospital, it still offered the rudiments of patient care. The authorities were obviously proud of it; an inspecting army officer seriously asked our senior medical officer if we had anything as nice as this in our country. It is possible the remark was more or less a barb rather than an inquiry. In comparison to what we had encountered as POWs it was indeed an improvement. To everyone's disgust, Nosu arrived one day to tell us he was still in command of all military prisoner hospitals in Kobe-Osaka (highly doubtful), and we were not to let anyone die here at Kobe — "I command!" This hospital undoubtedly was conceived as a propaganda effort in which the Japanese would seek endorsement from International Red Cross for the quality of treatment the Japanese were providing prisoners of war under their care.

Arriving from all prison camps in our part of Honshu, patients sent here were able to gather and evaluate the current news as it was being disseminated in various other camps. We at Kobe Hospital served as a clearinghouse for the news as well as a clearinghouse for the sick. The best source for rumor was "Kobe House," a British-American POW confinement located in the dock area where the prisoners were required to work as stevedores. These lads would feign a toothache or some other physical ailment in order to bring them to Kobe Hospital to exchange current news items. Their source of material was as factual as the propagandized edition of the Osaka-printed *Mainichi Shimbun's* interpretation of it could be relied upon.

Through contact with civilian laborers working alongside the Kobe House POW stevedores, a daily issue of the newspaper, printed throughout the war in English, was surreptitiously exchanged for food pinched by the POWs from the loading ships and warehouses. The Japanese workers, on a slow starvation diet themselves, were happy to exchange contraband material, especially when it involved food. Biased as the interpretation of the news might be, it was always possible to determine progress on the current major fronts.

We learned about the fall of Germany only a few days following VE Day. This news item, however, pointed out that the unfortunate loss of Japan's ally couldn't possibly affect the successful prosecution of the Greater East Asia war efforts. Naive, but of course no one took the comment seriously — not even their own *heitai* (soldier) who was guarding us. The *Mainichi* said they would fight on to the bitter end, and we carefully noted the terminology: the bitter end.

We appreciated *ocha* (tea) at Kobe during the winter months of 1944–1945. The temperature ranged from 0°F to 60°F, and a few sticks of *sumi* (charcoal) in a makeshift hibachi were issued to heat buildings in the evening where a Franklin-type, coal-burning stove might have had difficulty. Maybe ocha didn't raise the bodily heat materially, but it had great psychological merit, and we spent almost all our yen for tea. Even that became difficult to obtain toward the end: Japan was rapidly being forced into starvation-level food rations for all her people, and tea acreages were being converted into rice paddies. Food shortages were approaching a critical stage.

Ocha was consumed several times each day, or as often as our galley crew could find the extra wood for a fire to heat water. Obtaining firewood to prepare our meals became a serious problem as the war drew to a close. It even taxed the ingenuity of the guards, and very often those last days it amounted to scrounging with a guard and a two-wheeled cart at night, pilfering any private wood supply they (the guards) had spotted during the day — a not uncommon military procedure, or so it appeared. Apparently acquiring the wood in this manner eliminated the bothersome work necessary to procure it otherwise.

We were fortunate at Kobe in having Surgeon Lt. Comdr. John Page, Royal Navy, as senior POW officer. He was not only a "good troop," as the Australians put it, a "good bloke," as the British POWs expressed it, but also a "good shipmate" in GI terminology. He was fearless in approaching the Nipponese with complaints but used tactful and intelligent methods. By the time we arrived at Kobe, Dr. Akeroyd, our Ichioka group commander, had developed a very characteristic hacking, brassy cough, temperature elevation, and general malaise requiring that he become a bed patient. He remained a serious tubercular patient until the end of the war. We had some forty active tubercular cases, but now we could at least segregate them in a separate room.

In the fall of 1944 Dr. Ohashi told us we were to have a very important inspection at Kobe Hospital, so secret they couldn't tell us the nature of it in advance. We suspected, and correctly so, it would be an inspection by International Red Cross from Tokyo. Dr. Bernath of the Swiss consulate represented the interests of the two countries, Britain and America, and the Swedish consul, Bjoerstadt, a very pleasant fellow, came in the interest of the Dutch.

It so happened the day before they arrived that Cato went on a sadistic spree. Of late he had been temperate in his relations with us but on this occasion stepped back into character long enough to severely mutilate an American corpsman's face, blackening both eyes and disfiguring him otherwise. His appearance would be embarrassing to explain satisfactorily to the Red Cross visitors. The situation was resolved by Cato's being detailed by the guards to take Stradley outside the compound where he wouldn't be seen during inspection; we should like to have kept him around as a realistic example.

The Geneva representatives took the names of all POWs, assuring us our Kobe address would be forwarded to the Geneva Red Cross headquarters. After a fashion we were interviewed about our treatment, but we had to be very careful, for the colonel in charge had

Japanese interpreters within hearing at all times. We didn't wish to push our luck too far; after all, we were very much aware of being under control of the Japanese and not the International Red Cross for the remainder of the war — and we hadn't forgotten the effects of previous experiences, not entirely unrelated.

It was ironically amusing to have the quartermaster deliver several quarters of beef to our galley the day of the visit, prominently displaying them for the benefit of the inspection party. They were hurriedly removed when the party left the compound, in fact almost before the gate had closed upon their departure. Our real amazement, however, should have been that they were able to find several quarters of beef remaining in all of Japan.

We derived several benefits from the inspection, aside from meeting and talking with some of our own people who were not prisoners. The Japanese were satisfied with our conduct, at least to the extent that we had not created an embarrassing incident during the touchy interview, and in recognition of our favorable performance we were offered the privilege of making a radio speech to be broadcast to our homeland.

This interested us indeed, for we doubted our families had ever been given information about our welfare or status in any respect. We were allowed several days to prepare our 150-word messages; naturally the subject matter was restricted, and we had to use painstaking care in its preparation. In fact, the Japanese gave us several topics about which we had to talk regardless of what else we said.

I screened my message to Ila and Duane ever so thoughtfully; I had so much to tell them — a heart bursting — so much I should like to say that I wouldn't be permitted, and perhaps it would be the last opportunity ever to do so. On the day we made the recordings, with portable equipment brought in, we were under terrific emotional strain. I could visualize the occasion when Ila and Duane would listen to the rebroadcast at home, and it was upsetting for me picturing that day when I was speaking into the microphone in Kobe. They seemed nearer to me than at any time since I had been separated from them, yet in reality they were so terribly, terribly far away. This day was one of the most important of our stay in Kobe.

In the spring of 1945 we spaded a large portion of the yard to plant a vegetable garden. We gave Dr. Ohashi some yen for seeds, and he became quite enthusiastic about the whole project. Of course he assigned one of the guards to be in charge, a guard to whom we always had to look for advice, who was frequently not in agreement with us. He "advised" us to plant many *gobo*, which turned out to be an obnoxious burdock-like weed grown in Japan for greens, the black root cooked as a vegetable. It is neither tasty nor tempting in appearance, but it is easily grown in any type soil. We also were required to set out "much" eggplant; they are very fond of it, and when prepared with proper ingredients it is an appealing dish. Boiled in plain unseasoned water as flavoring for our soup it produced a sorry mess.

The Japanese are very partial to cucumbers, but cooking them (for health protection we had to cook all our vegetables) made cucumbers unpalatable. Interestingly enough, they used a climbing variety in Japan that had the added advantage of conserving valuable planting space. We told them we wanted to grow *takusan* (many) tomatoes; we all liked them, knew their value, and thought we might realize more of the harvested crop. We had previously determined that the Japanese as a rule do not relish them — they smell, we were told; we hoped their share of our tomatoes would be *sukoshi* (very little).

An unsavory feature of our garden was the huge amount of *daiben* (night soil) and urine we were obliged to apply to the various plots. The Japanese system of hilling and trenching keeps the material off the plants, but we were very apprehensive about the vast amounts used in such lava-type soil. We decided very early on we wouldn't under any circumstances eat our vegetables raw. The contents of the benjos from their guardhouses, as well as from our own dysentery-infected ones, were used. As distasteful as this aspect of Japanese gardening appeared to us, it was our observation that nothing of any value whatsoever is allowed to be wasted in Japan, in China, and throughout the entire Orient.

# Chapter 6

# To Tokyo on Impulse

The story of Smith's last months as a prisoner is framed by the growing realization of the imminent American victory, symbolized by the waves of B–29 bombers that flew over Japan almost unopposed. For the Japanese civilians the bombing raids were a shock. In their memory wars had always been fought on foreign soil; they had never seen modern warfare up close.

Precision bombing of industrial targets was the first strategy of the air force, as it tried to cripple Japan and take it out of the war, but the results had not proved satisfactory. In March 1945, when the Americans switched to using incendiary bombs against cities, the consequences were devastating. The first fire bombing raid against Tokyo, March 10, destroyed more than two hundred thousand buildings and killed more than eighty thousand people. Other cities came next, including Kobe and Osaka (it lost 60 percent of its buildings); both suffered so much destruction that they were eliminated as targets after two weeks of intensive bombing. So terrible was the destruction that the crews of the last waves of bombers that flew over some of these communities at elevations of 5,000 feet to 9,000 feet could smell the stench of burned flesh.

By August the end was near, and the dropping of the two atomic bombs brought the war to a close. Plans had already been made to rescue prisoners, and as soon as the cease-fire order of August 14 came, supply drops were initiated to the known camps. Planes made daily observation patrols to locate others.

"JAP WAR ENDED," the *Free Press* headlined the news on August 16. "Probably upper most in most minds was that thought that Lt. Stanley Smith may now be released." Early in September the family received two letters, one having been mailed back in June 1944, the other the preceding January; both were now anticlimactic (another one arrived even later, in October). Meanwhile, on a clear Sunday morning,

September 2, 1945, on the deck of the battleship *Missouri*, the surrender documents were signed. World War II was over.

The story comes to an incredible end with Smith's exciting trip to Tokyo to greet the incoming American forces and seek help for seriously ill prisoners. The adventure was reported by the *Chicago Daily News* (September 10, 1945), which was the first that the family and friends in Sandwich had heard about it.

Peace now returned to the little Illinois farming community and to the rest of the world. At the peak of enlistment 328 Sandwich men and women had been in service; six men had been killed in battle and two had been prisoners of war, the other in Germany. Stanley Smith returned to his hometown on Saturday, October 13, to spend the weekend with his family and to be greeted by relatives and friends. During his imprisonment, he had received very little news from home, only a few letters and one radio message; all that could be made up now. The years as a prisoner were behind him; the years of peace stretched out ahead.

### B-NI JU KU

St. Patrick's Day 1945 arrived like any other day, but a reminder of the evening's events will live with us for a long while. The air-raid siren down in Kobe sounded a long, wailing blast about midnight, and soon thereafter the short intermittent tones signaled the raid as bearing down on our locality. We had been cautioned what to do; all our stored sacks of rice had to be carried to the air-raid shelters we had previously prepared underground, our patients dressed and made ready to evacuate, etc. The raids prior to this one had been directed at nearby areas, avoiding Kobe. On this night General LeMay put on a fantastic aerial display for us. Apparently the Kawasaki Aircraft Factory at the edge of Kobe was one objective, but nearly a third of the whole factory area on the Kobe waterfront was heavily bombed with high explosives. Napalm was also used, but, in this raid, in limited areas.

It was the most spectacular and yet awesome sight we had so far been privileged to see. This was our first view of American planes using the new materials current for incendiary bombing, which was to prove so effective in certain parts of Japan. The guards gave us a bad time, knocking us around during the raid, but no one was seriously hurt and we were so elated nothing else mattered. The planes came in low over the area to avoid flak, and the fires set off by napalm clearly illuminated the insignia on the sides of the planes — we were thrilled! Above us were free Americans, the nearest contact we had made to any for more than three years; soon they would be returning to their base, probably having some good hot coffee and doughnuts on the way. The night's activity gave us a lift that lasted for many days.

*B-ni ju ku* (B–29) became a byword with every Japanese who was old enough to know and fear the result of its attack. The air siren sounded many times, almost daily now, so we were reasonably sure the mainland of Nippon was in the process of systematic destruction of the type we had just witnessed on the Kobe waterfront. The Japanese feared and hated the B–29s but at the same time grudgingly admired their beauty and efficiency; with all the antiaircraft fire the Japanese directed at them, very few deviated from perfect formation. It was most thrilling to those of us who were snatching a hasty look from behind black air-raid curtains.

An emphatic *"joto nai"* (not good) would be heard from the guards when the Kobe siren sounded in the distance; "B-ni ju ku *mudzukashii na"* (B–29 is very difficult). And how pleased we were to know they had become very difficult. Until now their activity had been occasional, but every day it was increasing in intensity, and after each raid in areas around us, we had to be very careful not to show how pleased we were. Our kiotsukes and *karis* (bows) were more painstakingly performed, more attention was given to our *arrigato* (thank you), our humble *gomen nasai* (excuse me, please) was more rigidly observed, and in all our contacts from now on we had to be on the alert: the Japanese remained in a nasty mood.

On several occasions when making trips with the guards into Kobe, using carts to obtain our quota of rice, barley, or millet, we were able to observe evidence everywhere of the extreme conditions being imposed upon the civilians. Poor, inadequate clothing and wan faces were a common sight. The Japanese were obviously feeling the effects of the food shortage, the threat of an attack, and war privations in general. Women and children were seen frantically digging air-raid shelters between and under their crowded frame-and-papier-mâché homes. It was depressing to navigate the streets, now virtually barren of motor traffic; it was also most interesting to note how completely the civilians ignored both the guards and us.

The military warehouses were located on the far side of the area so recently bombed, so we were able to see at close range the extent of the destruction as we walked through the two or three miles of flattened rubbish remaining along the waterfront. It sobered us, for the destruction was so complete we pondered our chances of survival when the time came to finish off the rest of Kobe with such carpet-bombing tactics.

We had nearly two-and-a-half months respite waiting for our famous B–29s to return in sufficient numbers to finish the job. In the meantime we went about our monotonous daily existence, watering and benjoing our garden, anxiously awaiting, however, the day when we could eat some of the tomatoes.

Everything in Japan seems to grow profusely because of their unusual fertilizing methods, but none of the few things we were ever privileged to consume appeared to have the delicious flavor of our stateside varieties. We had been denied such food for so long that our taste appreciation should have been especially sharpened, but we found the vegetables we had grown for the most part rather insipid. The Japanese produced many vegetables three times the size and beauty in outward appearance of ours at home, but any other favorable comparison could not be made. Our Kobe tomatoes became war casualties. We had some two hundred healthy plants, but I suspect the story would have been the same: tomatoes disappointing in taste.

Our garden was doing all right until the advent of the returning B–29s. Shortly after dawn on the morning of June 5, 1945, one could have observed our eggplants, cucumbers, and tomato plants gently waving in the warm summer breeze. The mournful air-raid siren broke the tranquility of the scene, heralding the arrival of what turned out to be about three hundred of our favorite long-range bombers, marking the end of so much of everything that to this moment had been alive and productive within a five-mile radius of the port area of Kobe. It proved to be the most spectacular, as well as one of the most terrifying, sights one could ever want to experience.

Graceful, silver birds, they appeared in a formation comprising waves of ten to twelve each, approaching nonchalantly from over the harbor of Kobe to begin the systematic destruction of a city totaling more than a million people. After frantically taking all the precautionary measures we could to insure the patients' and our own safety, we congregated at various points to witness, from our elevated position inland, the most frightening spectacle we had ever seen.

The swish of the bombs through the air, after we had watched their release from the bomb bays in such numbers as to resemble confetti, was a view to stagger the imagination. We had planned on, and been thrilled at the thought of, this devastating attack for more than three years — not, however, anticipating it would engulf us, as it would now appear it was about to do. At first we thought our hospital would escape; we were some three miles from the dock and in a completely residential area at the base of the mountains, slightly elevated from the rest of the city. As the raid grew in intensity and the waves of planes continued in relentless fury to sweep one strip at a time from the waterfront factories up the hill through the residential district, we realized we would lie in the direct path of this oncoming march of total destruction as the raid advanced in our direction.

After approximately two hours of siege, the billows of black smoke and flying debris had almost entirely obliterated the sun. It appeared now, when it could be seen at all, as a dark red ball of semimolten metal, strangely resembling the red flaming center of the Japanese flag. It wasn't safe to be outside the buildings, if one could be considered safe anyplace in this holocaust. Flying pieces of metal, burning timbers, and bits of shrapnel were everywhere in the air, blown about by a high-velocity wind created, I suppose, by the terrific currents of intermittent hot and cold air forming over the burning city.

On and on the planes came, and nearer ever nearer to us with each successive wave. With bombs bursting, antiaircraft shells exploding, screams and wails of the bewildered and trapped civilians rending the air, and pandemonium and chaos on all sides of us in this nightmare of destruction, our thoughts turned to the startling possibility that this would mark the end for all of us.

In a dazed manner we gathered in small groups around the various areas where bed patients had been placed in readiness for evacuation, when needed. While the group I was in stood on the porch outside what had been used as the surgical building, someone remarked, "As long as you hear the swish of the bombs coming through the air you are safe, for you never hear the string that hits you." Someone else said, "Here they come, duck!"

Would it be more advantageous to spend one's last few minutes alive inside or outside a particular building, was a question I am sure I did not weigh as I turned to walk aimlessly inside. It seemed natural, in retrospect, to want something over one's head at a time like this, and that is exactly what I got. When I had gotten a few feet inside the building, there was a blinding flash, a few seconds of semiblackout, and the superstructure of plaster, timbers, walls, and overhead completely covered me and continued to shower down, wedging me in.

Almost simultaneously, it seemed, a fire broke out directly ahead, and I realized being pinned in here would be a horrible death. Fighting desperately to free myself and to remove the dust and bits of debris from my eyes, I pushed, shoved, and climbed with all the energy I had. Fortunately during such periods our systems function beautifully with a superabundance of adrenalin to supply the necessary strength for the emergency at hand. I needed it that day to lift fallen beams and other heavy materials to free my way to the top and outside the pile of burning timbers.

One Australian corpsman had been pinned under too heavy a fragment for him to move, and his frantic cries as the fire approached were terrifying to hear. We managed to free him in time and then, cut, bruised, and distraught as we were, directed our effort toward carrying out patients who were unable to walk to comparative safety outside other burning buildings. Three patients were lost as the result of direct hits, and about thirty staff members and some thirty more patients received severe burns — a miraculously small percentage of casualties. We became immune to the noise and confusion of the continued bombing; our only concern was to escape to the nearby mountain before we would be cut off by the flames surrounding us on all sides.

Carrying our sick through the narrow, burning, back streets, praying to be granted a few minutes' grace before being trapped by the raging fires, we carefully made our way up the hill. Left to our own resources, the guards by now so panic-stricken themselves as to almost ignore our presence, we paused here and there to give what attention we could to the pitifully burned civilians along the way — brought to comparative safety by their friends. As I look back it seems strange there was no expression of resentment nor bitterness shown by these sufferers, some of them dying while receiving first aid. Others came to ask our assistance, although I am confident they realized we were in some way related to this calamity now engulfing them.

Numbed by the events of the last few hours, we sat the rest of the day at the base of the mountain watching Kobe burn as the fury of the bombing ceased. We returned late that evening to find complete destruction of our hospital and equipment. We stood among smoking embers to view without obstruction the miles upon miles of leveled rubbish that, just a few hours before, had been the homes and industry of nearly a million people.

After sleeping in the open in what had been the rather attractive enclosure of our Kobe hospital, we were told the next morning to assemble all who could walk for transfer to an abandoned camp about ten miles away; all others would be moved by vehicle. Our slow procession made its way through the charred and smoldering remains of the city now presenting an awesome picture in its destruction.

We found it necessary to detour here and there to avoid masses of tangled electric cables and the twisted steel girders of the tramway system destroyed with napalm incendiary bombs and twisted into oddly distorted shapes. We made our way past one small group after another digging among the rubble of tile roofing (all that remained of their highly inflammable little homes), trying to find cherished articles that might have withstood the flames. Silent, stoical people were these, who were carefully, reverently attempting to uncover the burned remains of family or friends who had died. So many had been trapped in the air-raid shelters they had prepared under and between their homes, citizens ill advised by the authorities, who should have provided better protection from inevitable incendiary attack.

They were pitiful, distressed groups, whose intense suffering showed so plainly in their bewildered faces and their silently bowed heads as they gave expression to their grief with remarkable control. Without experiencing the hopelessness of their tragedy, it was impossible for us to sense the full impact of the anguish tearing at their hearts as they looked down upon the disheveled array of smoldering ashes that such a short while ago represented the material wealth they had accumulated over an austere lifetime of endeavor.

There was never an expression of anger, nor any desire for revenge directed at our group as we slowly went on our way among them, we who were representatives of an enemy who yesterday had brought so much death and destruction to their homes, not one expression of hatred as we walked through the cluttered streets. They completely ignored our presence in their hour of grief. I wonder in what other area of the world, under similar circumstances, could one find such resolute self-control over such heartbreaking emotions? There was no outward expression of animosity, nor violent denunciation for what the most conservative among them must have regarded as a wanton and cruel attack.

The days at Kawasaki, our final destination, dragged on with increasing hardship and uncertainty. Our burned patients were given the best care available with limited, practically nonexistent medical supplies. Flies, fleas, and mosquitoes in droves were added to the discomforts with which we again had to cope. Our food, rice and millet, was reduced at one time to eight hundred calories per day. We served what little we received in two meals, preparing the grain as usual into a soft lugao. Inasmuch as the fresh water system in the area had been damaged in the raid, we now had to carry all our water into camp in large bamboo buckets, climbing a nearby hill to a well.

Several times daily the air-raid siren would sound, and often we would see large flights of planes in the distance and hear the rumble of exploding bombs. Throughout one night we heard heavy gunfire at sea, the sound easily distinguishable from bombing, and our thoughts turned to the possibility of a landing. We were told our stay here was temporary; they had no other place presently to put us. All other POW camps but one, Kobe House, had been moved from the area to distant mountains. We undoubtedly would have been moved except that our thirty-some active tubercular bed patients would have necessitated motor vehicle transportation requiring fuel not available, at least not to be expended on us.

We became depressed at Kawasaki. The trying ordeal of the Kobe disaster had helped deplete our diminishing reserve of strength, and I surmise our bodies had just about used up what little of everything we had left. We knew we were winning the war, but we also knew we were rapidly being drained of the stamina necessary to see us through to the end. Our environment, our food, and our health in general at Kawasaki were such that we were confident another winter in Japan under present hardships would wipe out the remaining POWs imprisoned there. So many could only be described realistically now as healthy-looking cadavers.

We had to persuade ourselves we were approaching a climax in the Asian conflict. It was inconceivable that Japan would fight on much longer against such odds and in the face of so much destruction and suffering now being brought home to it. We pinned our hopes on capitulation, for we believed a major Allied landing on the islands could be a death warrant for any remaining POW, who would then become an expendable nuisance. The *Mainichi Shimbun* cautiously reported that the enemy had used a highly destructive personnel bomb over Hiroshima. It went on to state, however, that such tactics would not in any possible way affect the successful outcome of Japan's efforts in the war. The Japanese government urged its people to persevere in the face of this newest threat.

Rumors coming to us from the guards were encouraging; they even dropped hints occasionally about current news. There was more deference shown in their relationship with us; they would now spend time in friendly conversation. They especially liked to discuss baseball in America, for it had become the most popular sport in Japan before the war. Some of these hopeful signs, I suspect, were the fruits of wishful thinking, but we soon were to know the answer.

### THE LONG-AWAITED PRONOUNCEMENT

With cautious optimism, arising mostly from desperation I presume, we waited outside Dr. Ohashi's office at noon on the 17th of August, 1945, where he had called the doctors for a conference. Each of us in his heart felt this was the day, the hour, the very moment we had been praying for, anxiously awaiting, anticipating since the fall of the Philippines. None of us wanted to disclose his innermost feeling; it was too intimate, a conviction we wanted to cherish without being challenged by someone less optimistic. The issue was too crucial after three-and-a-half years of continued disappointment and frustration. In reality we didn't need to be concerned about each other's thoughts; they were plainly expressed in our faces — we were of one opinion.

Emotional tension permeated the air and was apparent in everyone's actions as we entered the little wooden shack Dr. Ohashi used as his office. Upon seeing the Japanese doctor, we were satisfied he, too, was there under terrific strain. The pressure on us was a combination of elation and fear, fear that this conference we approached might not have been called for the purpose we had anticipated after all. The solemnity with which we were received as we made our entrance, the absence of the regular office force and guards, and the unusual atmosphere surrounding the whole procedure helped, however, to brighten the spark of hope so recently rekindled.

Dr. Ohashi, who usually appeared in his office wearing an undershirt and house slippers, now sat at his desk in full military regalia, patched, worn, and faded. We recalled not having seen him for several days, and we were quite shocked, but at the moment pleased, to see him looking so dejected, so completely emptied of any animation. The thought came to me as we lined up inside his office that surely this man looked representative of a nation thoroughly subdued and completely exhausted.

In broken English, haltingly, and obviously near the point of emotional breakdown over the words he was about to speak, in a voice hardly above a whisper, he stood with trembling hands holding a paper from which he read, "For you — I have good news; the war is now past!" This moment will never be forgotten as long as those of us who experienced the thrill of it shall live. The joyful thankfulness that overwhelmed us, the sudden release of all pent-up emotions of the past several years — it was almost too much for one to bear; truly our prisoner-of-war days had received God's blessing of a happy ending.

The gift of freedom, a priceless treasure eluding us for so long, we would soon enjoy once more. We had almost forgotten what it was like; we didn't know how to act, and surely some of us acted rather foolishly in an adventure we were about to take. If there is an explanation for it, perhaps it could be rationalized as a heady response to being suddenly released from restrictions so rigidly (we thought unjustly) imposed upon us for so long a period, a reaction to regaining a liberty we heretofore had accepted as our inalienable right, but which we now appreciated as something that sometimes had to be fought for, suffered for, and won before it could again be cherished and enjoyed.

## TO TOKYO ON IMPULSE

Yesterday we were prisoners of war under the Japanese in a foreign land. Today we were free, almost, and carried away with the knowledge of our liberation although still in a hostile environment, a factor we seemed to have overlooked in our exhilaration. Three of us were imbued with a perfectly ridiculous notion to go on a 250-mile journey to Tokyo to be there when General MacArthur and his advance forces arrived to sign the peace terms.

In every respect we were still POWs, but we thoughtlessly rationalized that from now on we would be responsible for our own welfare. Actually, the Japanese were now more than ever conscious of their responsibility for our safety and well-being until we were taken over by our own forces. In all fairness they could not be held entirely accountable for the projected journey over the countryside a few of us were contemplating without their permission.

After Dr. Ohashi's breathtaking announcement, we were granted the privilege of arranging our own liberty parties for hikes outside the camp into what was left of Kobe and the nearby areas. Our guards remained at the front gate, somewhat unsure about their role but assuming it had something to do with our protection. Two navy physicians, Berley and Glusman, and I went ahead with plans for our trip to Tokyo, scheduling our arrival there with that of the U.S. fleet.

Our friend and adviser, Dr. Page, the British surgeon, was rather restrained in his reaction, not at all enthusiastic about the plan. His comment, as I recall, referred to it as a "rum" idea. However, we expected our decision would be too impulsive for his British conservatism anyway. On the Saturday afternoon before MacArthur was to arrive in Tokyo, we put our adventuresome scheme into operation. Walking to the little Kawasaki station outside camp, we boarded the electric tram taking us into a Kobe railroad station, from which we hoped to secure transportation on into Tokyo. Our only luggage was some canned food from the parachuted supplies we had been receiving.

When hostilities terminated, Allied Command, as part of the cease-fire arrangement, required the Japanese to identify all POW camps in a manner so as to be plainly visible by Allied aircraft. Soon thereafter our planes began to parachute canned food in fifty-gallon drums to the POW areas. Weighted heavily, all too frequently these parcels landed in the living quarters of an unsuspecting homeowner after carving an opening through the roof. Wherever the food came to rest, the Imperial Japanese Command had warned civilians not to disturb it in any way. We in turn would be notified where the wayward drum with its precious contents had landed, and we would dispatch a party of POWs to retrieve it. The experience was delightful after three years and seven months on a rice diet of limited portions; however, no one enjoyed seeing civilian lives and homes endangered because of the practice.

We arrived about 5:00 P.M. at the Kobe railroad station, where it had begun to rain and blow. The unsettled weather should have dampened our enthusiasm to continue on, but unfortunately it didn't. After lengthy and rather difficult discussion with the surprised employee at the ticket office, we did finally manage to convince her we should be allowed to purchase transportation to Tokyo. Japanese civilians had been restricted because the military were utilizing every available passenger space for demobilization of their home army, hastily carrying out surrender directives.

Tokyo had been zoned, we were told; no one was allowed to enter except those with special military permits. Far from looking the part, we assured the agent we would qualify for such special consideration because we were American naval officers with an urgent mission we must fulfill in Tokyo. Our plan well might have failed completely had it not been for an English-speaking Japanese civilian who overheard our conversation in broken Nipponese and offered to present our qualifications more clearly to the somewhat bewildered agent.

His detailed explanation was the deciding factor. He then was helpful in telling us when our train was to leave and from which of the tracks. We would have to wait until 9:00 that evening, riding all night to arrive in Tokyo at 2:15 in the afternoon of the next day, Sunday. Everything so far seemed to be moving along with relative ease; our next objective was to board the 9:00 P.M. train going north.

Aware of all the unusual circumstances under which we would be traveling, it is difficult in retrospect for me to understand why we didn't just chuck the whole idea as a bit of impulsive nonsense. We were the only foreigners waiting to board the train; in fact, other than ourselves, there was no one to be seen anywhere on the platform except Japanese military, and we felt very much alone. Hundreds of uniformed soldiers, each carrying a pack, in some cases larger than themselves, literally covered the waiting area.

When the train arrived, each one fought his way madly to get aboard with his pack of bedding and nondescript gear. Doors provided the only orderly approach to the interior, but with combined pushing and wild jabbering at each other, they proceeded to swarm through the car windows, after first throwing in their packs. We didn't have any choice; we were literally shoved through a window along with this mob of soldiers eager to get home. We had become accustomed to crowded conditions with these people for the past three years, but never were we overwhelmed by such an avalanche of our former combatants.

Dr. Glusman and I got a seat alongside a soldier, the three of us facing three others, whose packs in the aisle supported three more soldiers on top. When the train finally got underway we found ourselves completely surrounded by these Asians in dirty, smelly uniforms. We of course were just as disheveled, equally as rough in appearance, and undoubtedly as offensive in every respect as our oriental companions in the stuffy car. We located Fred Berley in a seat directly behind us, where he, too, was equally enveloped by uniformed Japanese.

We presented an unusual picture, to say the least. After the turmoil subsided, we began to survey the situation around us: a trainload of returning soldiers who had accepted defeat at their emperor's request, bewildered, but until recently a very formidable adversary; a whole trainload of soldiers traveling with three former enemy naval officers crowded within their midst. We had to concede it wasn't an environment conducive to our personal welfare.

Glusman and I carried on a pleasant conversation with Berley in the seat directly behind us for some time, discussing our past experiences and reviewing things in general. It never entered our minds, in the confusion of voices surrounding us, that our passengers would be able to comprehend, or for that matter be at all interested, in what we were saying. We had been relatively comfortable for several hours when a soldier seated across from us said in perfect English, "You are POWs?" We had prepared ourselves for eventual interrogation, but didn't expect it here, so our somewhat startled reply informed him we were doctors, American navy doctors.

Japanese persistence being what it is, he pointedly but politely countered, "But you are POWs?" We could only answer that doctors, according to the Geneva Conventions, are never prisoners of war; we smugly thought we had a convincing rebuttal. Actually it was not entirely factual. However, one has to encounter a well-educated, English-speaking Japanese to appreciate fully how painfully tenacious he can be at times.

Our fellow traveler continued, "Then you have been, let us say, detained by the Japanese military?" We were suddenly aware how uncomfortably warm it was in the car, even with the open windows, but we replied we had been so detained, first in the Philippines, then in Kobe, Japan. "Ah yes," he went on with his logic well in hand, "Are you not then still to be considered under control of the military?" Those around us had stopped their noisy conversation and were staring at us seemingly for the first time. As our British friends would have said, there was a bit of strain in the air, but we didn't get the full significance at the time.

As POWs we had been closely associated with these people for more than three years, and although right at the moment we were in a position of even greater disadvantage, we had considerable experience behind us in handling them. With tongue in cheek we told him we were no longer considered prisoners in Kobe; we had been granted our liberty by Colonel Murata. The Japanese military had guaranteed our safety to General MacArthur (we rightly assumed it had been done), and now we were on an errand of mercy into Tokyo to contact our advance forces, who would arrive there tomorrow, seeking through them immediate transfer of our seriously sick POW patients who would soon die if not evacuated.

We were greatly relieved when this seemed to satisfy him, for he continued in a more friendly vein, "Now there is a typhoon approaching." (We had noticed the weather had increasingly worsened.) "The initial landing in Tokyo Bay has been delayed for two days." This news, if true, was very disquieting indeed, for we had timed our entry into Tokyo with the arrival of MacArthur's staff. We would be desperate for a place to stay if we arrived there ahead of them; we began to feel more than a little apprehensive about the whole adventure.

Obviously having no choice in the matter, we continued on our journey but made plans to meet whatever contingency awaited us in Tokyo. We encountered no further embarrassment from our inquisitive companions. The train arrived at our destination approximately on time. We had lost all returning soldiers at various stops along the way, and we were the only passengers still remaining aboard when the train pulled into Tokyo. Covered with soot, smoke, and dust blown in through the open windows as the coal-burning train slowly traveled the 250 miles through tunnels and over mountains, we made our way through the gutted remains of the once-beautiful Tokyo station.

The skies were overcast, with a blustering wind sweeping the area. Not another foreigner could be seen anywhere. In fact, there were very few Japanese on the streets that Sunday afternoon. What few there were, walking or riding bicycles, turned to stare at us as we ambled down the center of the street. We anxiously scanned the immediate area hoping to see other liberated POWs, as we had been observing them on the streets of Kobe.

Having been convinced of MacArthur's delay in arrival because of weather conditions, we had reluctantly formulated an alternate plan. We would go to the Imperial Hotel — Berley and I had been there before the war — and if it were still in operation we would no doubt find someone speaking English employed there. In case it had been destroyed by air attack, we would seek the Swiss legation and Dr. Bernath, who had visited us at Kobe Hospital.

Ours was a perplexing dilemma, for it was apparent to us now that POWs, in Tokyo at least, had not been granted special privileges as we had succeeded in persuading the authorities at Kobe-Osaka to give. It was also apparent, from the surprised and equally grave expression on the faces of civilians we passed, that they were not at all convinced our presence on their deserted streets was by proper authority. Is it any wonder they would be astonished and perturbed to encounter us as we appeared that Sunday afternoon, considering time and place and under the prevailing circumstances?

No one attempted to detain us, however, and some of those we tried to apprehend to verify directions ignored us completely. It was embarrassing and most frustrating, but the Japanese had been making things embarrassing for us for three and a half years, and we were quite accustomed to it. Walking through their almost deserted city for quite some distance, we eventually became concerned about the direction we were taking. Our uncertainty grew, and we finally had to hail a lone military truck appearing with two soldiers in it. The military, we felt confident, would know how to direct us and perhaps offer the safest protection in the event we were required to identify ourselves.

The truck's occupants seemed to understand our query about the Imperial Hotel and were apparently satisfied we had sufficient reason to be taken there. We were relieved to climb aboard, getting off the streets and thus becoming less conspicuous to the staring gaze of the civilians. The hotel, save one wing damaged by the bombing, appeared outwardly to be in satisfactory condition. The exterior looked neglected, but almost everything in Tokyo gave evidence of the war's dwindling economy. Building after building we had passed had only walls to cover the rubble of a gutted interior. The streets of Tokyo, in contrast with other Japanese cities we had recently been in, were spotless; apparently every effort had been made to eradicate evidence of the extensive destruction caused by the countless B-29 raids.

The Japanese lorry, with its strange cargo of three disheveled U.S. Navy officers, turned into the main entranceway of the Imperial, where we were deposited without interference. We had resigned ourselves to the possibility of being brought to a Kempi interrogation center for questioning, so we were greatly relieved. Looking like bums from the wrong side of the tracks in our filthy attire and soot-covered faces, we boldly walked into the lobby of this very attractive hotel designed by Frank Lloyd Wright.

The rugs and draperies in the hotel were beginning to present a worn and faded appearance, but everything else was just about as I remembered it from when I had come ashore here in 1940. We stepped up to a very properly dressed but now somewhat bewildered Japanese clerk at the desk and asked, as officers of the United States Navy, to register for room and board during the next several days. As in prewar days, when by reputation it was customary for the Japanese to show tactful diplomacy to strangers almost approaching servility at times, our clerk, with the characteristic sudden intake of breath, proceeded to give us some disquieting information.

At present they were preparing the hotel for occupancy by the new Foreign Office that was to meet with General MacArthur's staff. Therefore it was difficult to grant our request as the need for rooms was excessive, but would we be seated in the lobby and he would do whatever was possible for us. He readily agreed to show us where we might clean up a bit; upon our return we were directed to some comfortable chairs in the balcony surrounding the foyer. We felt confident it was a brush-off until he could notify the Kempi military police or the Foreign Office of this most unusual situation.

Soon a soft-spoken individual, Fujisaki, one of the secretaries in the Foreign Office, arrived with his pencil and notebook in hand to ask the endless questions prompted by the suspicious circumstances surrounding our presence. The Foreign Office found it hard to believe we had safely completed our journey from a Kobe POW camp to Tokyo by train. He said there were two things that led him to this conclusion. First, we were still POWs and as such hadn't been officially liberated from under the control and protection of the Japanese military. Second, he thought it incredible for three of us to risk boarding a train, especially one crowded with returning soldiers harboring mixed emotions, and come all this distance unattended. He reminded us how we unwittingly had exposed ourselves to fanatical elements with real suicidal potentialities, fanatics who were still in evidence all along the route we had traveled.

"Didn't people throw stones at you, stare at you, attempt to molest you? We are daily confining hundreds of avowed fanatics who would gladly have taken your lives in one last gesture of revenge." He proceeded to paint a rather grim picture, but the fact remained we had arrived safely, somewhat bedraggled and hungry, but nevertheless in reasonable soundness of body, so we reminded him his concern was somewhat anticlimactic. We were hungry; would they please get us some food for which we would expect to pay, and would they see to our comforts until we could deliver in person our message to General MacArthur concerning our errand of mercy? We thoroughly enjoyed using the general's name in our conversation with them now; during the war as POWs we dared not bring it into any discussion. The favorable response it presently brought forth was most refreshing.

They served us our first complete meal in three-and-a-half years. We enjoyed breaded veal cutlets, fresh vegetable salad, rice prepared like we had never had it as POWs, and some fresh bread and butter, with hot tea and rice cakes for dessert. They provided us with a room where we enjoyed a hot bath in proper surroundings and comfortable beds and chairs — we went from one to the other trying them out. Such luxury — in more than three years we had almost forgotten what it was like. As POWs we had traveled a long, rough road and lost many of our friends along the way, but the immediate amenities we were relishing had not been affected by the events of the past several years.

There were still a few differences to be resolved, and the Foreign Office remained in control of our movements for the next several days. We had refused (a word we hadn't used in conversation with them for more than three years) to return to Kobe as they had tried to persuade us to do, promising as an inducement to deliver our message of urgency to General MacArthur. We were beginning to enjoy ourselves thoroughly, especially when we realized they were concerned about our welfare. This strengthened our determination, and where we had been reserved in our appeal, we now assumed a more adamant stand, demanding the privilege of contact with our own military. We reminded them the war was over.

For three days, while occupying a suite without charge at the hotel, with all meals served in our rooms or on a balcony overlooking the rest of the city, this wrangling interrogation and persistent argument by the Kempi and Foreign Office continued. They assigned us a guard for our protection, as well as an interpreter, both occupying an adjoining room and always polite enough to announce themselves before entering ours.

Mr. Kiyoaki Nakao, the interpreter, was a Japanese schoolteacher educated at Catholic University, Dayton, Ohio, who only recently had been drafted into Kempi military duty. His outstanding ability as an interpreter was to be used in the forthcoming Allied Conferences. He visited with us in our room most of the time, fanning himself in true Japanese fashion and bringing us up-to-date for the first time with actual events since the war began. We were introduced to such innovations as rockets, sonar, and radar. He provided us with the names of all the American planes we observed zooming overhead in Tokyo, their pilots for all the world acting like a bunch of school kids chasing each other at play. We really enjoyed our stay at the Imperial Hotel as guests of the Japanese, in spite of all the annoying frustrations.

From our balcony on Tuesday we watched the arrival of the vanguard of the Allied staff, the big transport planes landing in the vicinity of Atsuji Airport. We waited all day to be taken for our initial contact with them, as our benefactors had at one time reluctantly indicated might happen, but we waited in vain. Finally, at 5:00 P.M., as we were enjoying the food served in our room, the foreign secretary, who had originally interviewed us, came in with his final instructions. They were sorry, very sorry, but the Foreign Office had decided against allowing us at present to contact the advance Allied contingent arriving in Tokyo. He said he had done everything possible for us to present our case in a favorable manner.

We told him we were extremely disappointed and implied by so doing that the Foreign Office could perhaps be instrumental in causing further loss of American lives, which would be its responsibility. Had we been willing to face it at the time, this was an exaggeration on our part, but we were feeling so important in assuming the role of conqueror for a change. Amusingly, our attitude didn't in the least ruffle Mr. Foreign Secretary, but I suspect he would have enjoyed being free to express his real thoughts about the matter.

Asked whether those at the Foriegn Office could give a reasonable explanation for their decision he said they believed our mission was admirable, but in their opinion the risk and danger involved in our breaking POW camp unauthorized and traveling all this distance from Kobe unattended must have been prompted by some ulterior motive. Our most unorthodox conduct, he continued, must have originated from some unpleasant POW experience, prompting us to interview General MacArthur before the signing of the terms of surrender. "Possibly was it your intention to inform him of your interpretation of prisoner atrocities perpetrated during the war, thereby attempting to influence him in some manner that would impose more severe penalties upon the Japanese people? When the agreed terms of the surrender have been signed you will be taken immediately to MacArthur's headquarter."

Incredible as it sounded to us at the time, we realized what we were experiencing was entirely within the framework of his reasoning; he repeated it in all soberness and sincerity. After all, our stories of maltreatment would surely have had a sympathetic ear with our command, and we weren't loath to tell them, but their importance was obviously insignificant in the course of events on the USS *Missouri*.

We realized our backs were against the wall, any further discussion pointless, and so we requested to be taken to the office of the Swiss consul, where we would complete our mission with Dr. Bernath. There, in the American Embassy Building presently being used by the Swiss, we spent our first pleasant evening among friends, enjoying the hospitality of the consulate staff. Here once again were lovely soft carpets and comfortable appointments of all description. We tasted refreshing soft drinks and delicious food served in a manner that as POWs we used to dream about, wondering what the odds might be of ever again enjoying them. Dr. Bernath invited as many other associates as he could reach, including the Swedish consul (Bjoerstadt) we had liked so well on his visit to Kobe and several assistant secretaries, and together they proceeded to make it a delightful evening we would long remember.

Our friends reviewed the main events of the war, the terms of the surrender, and other interesting items about which we had not heard. Without fear of reprimand or reprisal we now could freely and openly discuss any subject. The Japanese foreign secretary sat around in understandably glum silence; one could hardly expect the poor man to enter into any spirit of celebration.

What an exhilarating future was unfolding: no more rice or stale boiled fish, no more daikons, no more bango, slapping, pushing, bowing. How can one, in all justice to the occasion, describe the wonderful feeling of release from such an unAmerican way of life? Dr. Bernath took the names of our immediate family to whom messages of assurance could be sent and promised to deliver our request to Allied headquarters for air evacuation of our tubercular patients.

Walking back to the hotel with the secretary and the guards who had been required to await our arrival outside the embassy, we told them we were now very willing to return to Kobe and the slower processes of liberation. Our train ride the next day was more dignified, as crowded as ever, but seats were made available for us by the Kempi guard and interpreter who rode with us to assure our safe delivery to proper POW authority.

And so we returned to Kobe after a most hilarious and, I am sure, unparalleled experience of being the first Americans, liberated and free in almost every sense of the word, to enter Tokyo on their own after the cessation of hostilities. Our escapade was documented in an edition of the *Chicago Daily News*, but the significant emotional involvement surrounding the whole adventure will, for the most part, always remain locked up in our hearts — where I suspect it belongs.

The days slowly dragged on until our liberation by the occupational forces. Although stateside food and clothing were dropped by parachute almost daily from army and navy planes flying over the area, our continued confinement under the Japanese until September 8 seemed interminably long. The food, so rich and plentiful, was too much for our grain-adjusted constitutions. After the first several days of engorgement, patients as well as staff were anxious to return temporarily to the simple rice diet our digestive systems had adjusted to during our POW days. We did enjoy the realization that other food was available and the fact that it was a part of the life to which we were returning. What mattered ever so much more than food was the assurance of our going home. Sometimes we were almost afraid it was a dream, afraid we would awaken again to the grim reality of continued prisoner-of-war existence.

The fulfillment of a desire uppermost in my mind throughout my entire prisoner-of-war confinement that I anticipated would be the most exciting moment of my life was about to be realized. I was going home to my precious family: my wife, Ila, and our little son, Duane, whom in August 1940 I left as a small lad of three and a half years to report to the Asiatic Fleet. How would I appear to them, what changes had this nightmare of experience brought about in me that perhaps might influence their lives, what changes had the war brought about in them — in everything? Throughout the long and seemingly endless days of our POW sojourn I had always felt that we who were fortunate enough to survive would at its end pass through three of the greatest emotional experiences of our lives. The first would be the devout thankfulness when first we knew the war had ended. The second would be the unrestrained excitement and emotional pride engulfing us when we stepped ashore once again on American soil. However, by far the most thrilling and satisfying of all, an emotional experience the height of which we undoubtedly would never again attain in our lives, would be the overwhelming joy welling up within us when we were once again in the presence of those who were nearer and dearer to us than anyone or anything else in this world.

The termination of the war, my voyage home from Yokohama on the USS *Rescue*, and my first glimpse of Golden Gate Bridge, then hearing Ila's and Duane's voices for the first time over long-distance telephone from San Francisco, convinced me these contemplations cherished throughout those years of turmoil were indeed realistic.

Finally, my reunion with them at home further persuaded me that surely this blessing, which it was my extreme pleasure to experience, is deserving of a lifetime of thankful appreciation. I should like to dedicate myself to realizing this conviction.

# Epilogue

Stanley W. Smith was home to stay, his prisoner-of-war experiences now a gradually fading memory. For meritorious service and valor, he was awarded the Purple Heart Medal, the Bronze Star, and the Gold Star in lieu of a second Bronze Star.

In December 1945 he received a letter from President Harry Truman, which said, in part: "You have fought valiantly and have suffered greatly. As your Commander in Chief, I take pride in your past achievements and express the thanks of a grateful Nation for your services in combat and your steadfastness while a prisoner of war." It was a fitting tribute to his past four years.

In a Memorial Day address in 1895 Oliver Wendell Holmes, Jr., aptly expressed the feelings of those who had participated in war: "As for us, our days of combat are over. Our swords are rust. Our guns will thunder no more. . . . We have shared the incommunicable experience of war; we have felt, we still feel, the passion of life to its top."

# Further Readings

For those interested in pursuing the subject of American prisoners of war in the Pacific during World War II, the following books are recommended. E. Bartlett Kerr, *Surrender and Survival: The Experience of American POWs in the Pacific, 1941–45* (New York: William Morrow & Co., 1985) provides the best overview and includes an excellent bibliography.

Several first-hand accounts overlap Stanley Smith's. Thomas Hayes, *Bilibid Diary* (Hamden, CT: Archon Books, 1987) is one of the best. Calvin E. Chunn, ed., *Of Rice and Men* (Los Angeles: Veterans Publishing Co., 1946) reflects the bitterness of the immediate postwar era. John M. Wright, Jr., *Captured on Corregidor* (Jefferson, NC: McFarland & Co., 1988) recounts his Bilibid and Cabanatuan experiences. Ben Waldron, *Corregidor, "From Paradise to Hell"* (Freeman, SD: Pine Hill Press, 1988) and Manny Lawton, *Some Survived* (Chapel Hill, NC: Algonquin, 1984) add their remembrances.

To set the general scene, Samuel Eliot Morison, *The Two-Ocean War* (New York: Little, Brown & Co., 1963) and John Toland, *The Rising Sun: The Decline and Fall of the Japanese Empire* (New York: Random House, 1970) are recommended. The fall of the Philippines is examined in detail in Morison's *The Rising Sun in the Pacific* (Boston: Little, Brown & Co., 1948) and Louis Morton's *The Fall of the Philippines* (Washington, D.C.: Government Printing Office, 1953). Morison's *Victory in the Pacific 1945* (Boston: Little, Brown & Co., 1960) traces the last months of the war. The Japanese perspective may be found in Saburo Ienaga, *The Pacific War* (New York: Pantheon, 1978) and Akira Iriye, *Power and Culture* (Cambridge, MA: Harvard University Press, 1981).

# Index